A WILTSHIRE PARSON AND HIS FRIENDS

A WILTSHIRE PARSON
AND HIS FRIENDS

THE CORRESPONDENCE OF
WILLIAM LISLE BOWLES

TOGETHER WITH FOUR HITHERTO
UNIDENTIFIED REVIEWS BY COLERIDGE

EDITED BY

GARLAND GREEVER

BOSTON · AND · NEW YORK
HOUGHTON MIFFLIN COMPANY

First Published in 1926

Printed in Great Britain at
The Mayflower Press, Plymouth. William Brendon & Son, Ltd.

TO
GAMALIEL BRADFORD

Macpherson and intended indirectly for Thomas Gray), one from Campbell, one from Joanna Baillie, one from Amelia Opie, one from Sydney Smith, one from Barry Cornwall, two from Milman, two from Montgomery, about forty from publishers and editors, seventy-nine from the Lansdownes, and a number from other persons. I need hardly state that this collection constitutes my greatest single " find " and supplies a large part of the material for the present volume.

The Pentre Mawr Collection, still undispersed, is in the hands of Mrs. Herbert Jones-Bateman. Of all other collections and materials I must speak in the past tense, since my definite knowledge of them ceases after 1914–15. John Murray, Esq., had in his possession fifty-nine letters written to his grandfather and his father by Bowles, and one to Rogers by Bowles. These he generously placed at my disposal. Miss Warter, of Sidbury, owner of Southey's correspondence with Caroline Bowles, had six letters from Bowles to his " namesake " which she kindly consented that I should publish. Gordon Wordsworth, Esq., of Ambleside, was in possession of the two letters from Bowles to his grandfather which, through his liberality, are incorporated in this volume. Fairness demands of me the statement that in each of these instances the decision as to how much material I should include or exclude rested solely with myself.

J. Rogers Rees, Esq., of Merrixton House, Pembrokeshire, had, along with miscellaneous letters, a considerable number of communications which passed between Bowles and Nichols, a long and cordial letter from Bowles to Christopher North, and the manuscript of Bowles's account in the *Gentleman's Magazine* for June, 1835 (printed there with some alterations) of his first meeting with Coleridge. This material Mr. Rees freely permitted me to examine. Two smaller collections I was prevented, by an unfortunate

might normally seek them; the great majority, however, have existed far aside from the beaten ways of
scholarship. Rarely have any found their way into
the manuscript collections of libraries. Of the few
preserved in the British Museum I have selected only
one, that of May 26, 1832, concerning Disraeli.
The Harvard Library, since I consulted it, has
acquired a number, including two to Caroline Bowles
and twelve or fifteen to Pickering and Mitford.
Through the courtesy of Mr. Alfred C. Potter, the
Assistant Librarian, and the friendly help of Mr.
Gamaliel Bradford, I am able to reproduce the two
most important—that directed to Caroline Bowles on
November 9, 1823, and that directed to Mitford in
Pickering's care on April 8, 1836.

Of all the other letters here printed, the originals
were, when I examined them, in private hands.
Bowles's own papers might appropriately be styled
the Pentre Mawr Collection because they were placed
in the family library at Pentre Mawr, Abergele, by
the poet's niece Mrs. Jones-Bateman (born Marianne
Burlton), and remained there until shortly before the
outbreak of the recent World War. Bowles's niece
bequeathed them to her son the Reverend Burlton
Jones-Bateman, from whom they descended to the late
Herbert Jones-Bateman, Esq. Through Herbert
Jones-Bateman, Esq., then living at Eyarth, North
Wales, I obtained access to them; and I should indeed
be ungrateful if I failed to record his generosity in grant-
ing me unrestricted use of the material, his assistance
in various other ways, or his great personal kindness.
The Pentre Mawr Collection comprises, in addition
to manuscripts and sundry documents, two letters
each from Coleridge and Sheridan, nine each from
Rogers and Crabbe, twenty-eight from Moore, fourteen from Southey, seven from Caroline Bowles,
one from Madame de Staël, one from Landor, one
from David Hume (the often-cited one relative to

degree Rogers', are like the crisp salutations of well-bred men who reserve fuller discourse for hours of leisure. The correspondence with the Lansdownes has a sociological bearing, and that regarding *The Missionary* affords insight into publishing conditions.

In most instances I have placed in one group the letters of each of Bowles's correspondents. But it has not always seemed best to adhere to this arrangement. Thus Southey's letters are dispersed among three groups. The index may be used in tracing the activities of any given writer.

I have tried so to edit the letters as to make them attractive enough for general readers and yet accurate enough for scholars. For the sake of uniformity, I have set the date and address of the sender at the beginning of the letter, even though the sender himself had placed them last. The address of the recipient I have omitted except when there was evidence that it was not his usual address. A few unimportant postscripts I have, without warning, struck out. I have silently corrected a few misspellings and a few obvious slips of the pen; at the same time I have respected the writer's preferences in such words as " honour," " honor "—even when his preferences went both ways. I have expanded, in the body of the letters, such abbreviations as " wd " for " would," " Mag." for " Magazine," and " Q. R." for *Quarterly Review*. I have to a considerable extent modernized the punctuation and the use of capitals, though preserving, so far as I have been able, individualities which do not clash too sharply with present usage. Finally, I have printed awkward and even ungrammatical expressions just as they were written, without interjecting the sapient but officious *sic*.

It remains for me to indicate the sources of my material and to acknowledge the permissions and the help which have been extended me. Some of the letters have long been in places where the investigator

PREFACE

Most of the letters included in this volume I discovered in the year 1914–15, when I was in England as Sheldon Fellow from Harvard University. A few of them have come to my attention subsequently.

All the letters concern themselves in one way or another with William Lisle Bowles. In the Introduction, therefore, I discuss briefly the life of this poet-clergyman, his literary works, and his relationships with various contemporaries. In the notes I supply further details. But I have not attempted a formal biography. This I reserve until I have leisure to revise, in biographical form, the dissertation on Bowles which I prepared during my candidacy for the Ph. D. degree at Harvard.

With but two exceptions the letters in the present volume have been until now unpublished. They vary in importance. Most precious of all are the two from Coleridge. These tell us a few things we did not know before regarding the composition of the tragedy *Osorio* (later called *Remorse*), and reveal Coleridge's authorship, hitherto unsuspected, of important contributions to the *Critical Review*. Interesting too is the letter, long lost, which Southey wrote at the time of Coleridge's death and which, from Moore's reference to it, has been known to be of consequence in determining the laureate's final attitude to his old associate. The letters relative to the controversy with Byron reveal much of the secret history of that mêlée of criticism. Crabbe's letters are expressive of his good humor and his loneliness ; Moore's, and in less he was devoted to everything musical; and when as a young man he began to write sonnets, he made allusion to these very bells:

> "When, from an ancient tow'r, ere life's gay prime,
> The mournful magic of their mingled chime
> First woke my wond'ring childhood into tears."

The boy was William Lisle Bowles. He was then in his seventh year.

On a still night the travelers approached Uphill, and as a low murmur met their ears, Bowles's mother said softly, "Listen! it is the sea!" The lad "closer pressed her hand." When his eyes beheld Bristol Channel the next morning, the impression was one that he never forgot.

The living at Uphill had been obtained through John Willes, grandfather of the future Lady Beaumont. William Thomas Bowles, whose father and grandfather had been clergymen before him, was a kindly man, with a keen eye for natural scenery, and a fondness for planning walks and planting shrubs in his acre and a half of parsonage ground. His wife, herself the daughter of a clergyman, loved sacred music, revered Young's *Night Thoughts* "next to God's own word," and drew tears from the eyes of her children by reciting to them the story of Robinson Crusoe, "that desolate wild man" with "the speaking bird."

At Uphill Bowles spent a boyhood which, in its alternation of animal impulse with solemn emotional joy, was not unlike Wordsworth's. His school tasks, it is true, he did not perform with much pleasure. But his mood was rapturous when he "pursued the colts among the sand-hills"; launched "his pumpkin-ship, new-rigged and buoyant," on the garden pond; or, on an occasional visit to Wells Cathedral, beheld the horsemen of the clock gallop in tourney. From the eminence on which stood the church of Uphill, and at the foot of which nestled the village, he could

A WILTSHIRE PARSON AND HIS FRIENDS

INTRODUCTION

I

THE LIFE OF WILLIAM LISLE BOWLES
(1762–1850)

ON the afternoon of the eighth of May, 1769, two chaises were ready to set out from the Angel Inn at Bristol, before which they had drawn up only a short time before. The chaises contained the family and servants of a clergyman who had just been promoted from the living at King's Sutton, Northamptonshire, to that of Uphill and Brean in Somerset. The booted postilion looked back to see if all was right, and the travelers prepared to climb to their places, when somebody cried, " Where is Billy ? "

" Merciful heaven ! " exclaimed the mother of the family, " where is that boy ? "

A search was instantly begun, servants were sent out, passersby were questioned. Fortunately the boy might be easily identified, for he was arrayed " in a new white hat, the crown encompassed with a stripe of gold lace, in a sky-blue jacket, and neat pair of Banbury-fair boots." After a time he was found seated peacefully on the steps of St. Mary Redcliffe Church, listening in delight and wonder to the peal from the old tower. He had heard the sound of the bells the moment the chaises had stopped at the Angel, and had immediately wandered away. The incident is characteristic of him, for throughout his long life

B

CONTENTS

enumerate them all is impossible. But I cannot forbear to name some. Miss Marian Jones-Bateman has been zealously interested in my researches, and her good offices have been invaluable to me. Mrs. Herbert Jones-Bateman, Miss Margaret Jones-Bateman, Professor George Lyman Kittredge, the late Professor William A. Knight, and my wife have each extended substantial assistance. I acknowledge, last of all, great indebtedness to the scholar under whom my study of Bowles was begun—Dr. William A. Neilson.

conjunction of circumstances, from seeing. Ernest Jones-Bateman, Esq., of 11 Portland Avenue, Exmouth, Devonshire, had three letters from Bowles to John Scott; and the late A. M. Broadley, Esq., of Bridport, had a number from Bowles to Crabbe. Mr. Jones-Bateman has since disposed of his letters, and those owned by Mr. Broadley have probably been dispersed.

My obligations do not end with present or recent owners of the letters. I am equally indebted to kinsmen and legal representatives of the writers, whose kindness I have experienced and whose rights I fully acknowledge. I have named some of these persons already. I now have the pleasant task of expressing my thanks to the others. Permission to publish material has been accorded me by the late E. H. Coleridge, Esq., of Aylesbury (the letters of Coleridge); Mrs. James Orr of 26 Warwick Road, Earl's Court, and Miss Mary Crabbe of 5 St. George's Place, Brighton (the letters of Crabbe); Lady Agatha Russell of Rozeldene, Hindhead (the letters of Moore); Algernon Brinsley Sheridan, Esq., of Frampton Court, Dorchester (the letters of Sheridan and Linley); Miss Matilda Sharpe of 32 Highbury Place (the letters of Rogers); Viscount Knutsford of Kneesworth Hall, Royston, Hertfordshire (the letter of Sydney Smith); the Marquess of Lansdowne (the letters of his grandfather and grandmother); Messrs. Pickering and Chatto (the letters of Pickering); and Messrs. William Blackwood and Sons (the letter from the editor of *Blackwood's Magazine*). In a few instances I have been unable to come in touch with descendants or personal representatives of the writers of letters, but because the letters are of a nature so thoroughly inoffensive have ventured to include them anyhow.

There are many persons, finally, from whom I have received aid of a kind difficult to specify. To

see for miles across the low country, and even look down the coast to the region which was afterwards to be associated with the composition of the *Lyrical Ballads*. Wandering along the winding sands of the shore, he listened to " the sea-gull warping on the wind "; dreamed of faraway climes while he gazed at the solitary vessel that hung motionless " between sea and sky "; or merely watched

> " The long waves, breaking slow, with such a sound
> As Silence, in her dreamy mood, might love."

As the years passed, other interests developed. Once, when he had come back from Oxford, he strolled forth in the early morning with scarcely better hope than to find some fisherman dredging for shrimps. Instead

> " I beheld—or was it not
> A momentary vision ?—a fair form—
> A female, following, with light, airy step,
> The wave as it retreated, and again
> Tripping before it, till it touched her foot,
> As if in play; and she stood beautiful,
>
> .   .   .   .   .   .
>
> Graceful, and young, and on the sands alone."

He vowed in his heart eternal love, but was too diffident to do more than " cast a parting look "; whereat

> " The vision smiled,
> And left the scene to solitude."

He saw her only once thereafter.

Before the death of William Thomas Bowles in 1786 the family began to spend some part of each year in Barton Hill House, Shaftesbury. Bowles attended a school there; also " for a short time when young " he had a " course of education at Strasbourg." In 1775 he was elected scholar of Winchester College, though his name does not appear on the books of the

institution until the next year. He remained at
Winchester until 1781, in which year he also gained
a gold medal for a Latin essay. He liked his associates
at Winchester, of whom Howley, the future Archbishop of Canterbury, was one. He must also have
been pleased with the shilling, the Sunday dinner,
and the glass of wine he obtained each week from his
great-uncle who was fellow there. Best of all, he came
under the influence of the headmaster, Joseph Warton,
who awakened his faculties, encouraged him to write
verse, and gave definite bent to his literary ideals.
From Warton he borrowed a distrust of Pope, and
acquired or augmented his love of nature, of the
ancient classics, of Shakespeare, of Ossian, of Milton
and unfettered verse, and of Warton's own poems,
especially the " Ode to Fancy." It was fitting that
afterward, when Warton died, Bowles should pay
him an affectionate tribute; for Warton made Bowles
a poet, made him moreover a romantic poet.

It is customary for Winchester men to enroll at
New College, Oxford; but as Bowles's name was
eighth on the list sent up in 1781, he did not secure
a vacancy, and matriculated at Trinity College instead.
The following year he was elected to a scholarship
that did not expire until 1787. " He also held the
' Cobden ' exhibitioner awarded to a Trinity man
educated at Winchester, 1785-9." It has been said
that he chose Trinity College because Thomas Warton
was a senior fellow there. By Warton's sonnets and
interest in mediaeval subjects he must have been
considerably influenced. Several of his friends among
the students were young men of literary taste; in
particular we may note William Benwell, Henry
Headley, and Thomas Russell. Bowles himself won
in 1783, with his " Calpe Obsessa," or " The Siege
of Gibraltar," the chancellor's prize (of £20) for
Latin verse.

He received his A. B. in 1786. A long absence

at the beginning of the following autumn, and another at the beginning of 1787, were apparently due to the death of his father. After July, 1797, his name ceases to appear in the records of the college. As he held the Cobden exhibitioner, however, until 1789, and appears to have been in residence during the latter part of 1788 and for some months thereafter, he probably maintained an intermittent connection with Oxford. A letter written by his mother in 1788 explains that he was hoping for a fellowship. He obtained his A. M. in 1792.

Meanwhile, not earlier than 1785, it would seem, and not later than 1788, an event of great importance had befallen him. He had become engaged to a young lady, said to be a niece of Sir Samuel Romilly; but she had broken the engagement, apparently at the command of her parents, who regarded his prospects as uncertain. Bowles sought solace in travel. His excursions, at first confined to the North of England and Scotland, were finally extended to Antwerp, along the Rhine, and into Switzerland. The future Earl of Cork and Orrery was his companion during at least the journey along the Rhine. During these rambles Bowles composed a number of sonnets, which were suggested by the scenes before him: " whenever such scenes appeared to harmonise with his disposition at the moment, the sentiments were involuntarily prompted." He did not write them down at the time; but later, in an hour of financial need, committed fourteen of them to writing, and offered them to Richard Cruttwell, a printer of Bath. One hundred copies were issued in 1789, and a second edition of five hundred copies (the number of sonnets being increased to twenty-one) was called for the same year. This supplied the demand until 1794, but by 1805 no fewer than nine editions had been published. Apart from a sonnet and some " Verses to the Memory of Henry Headley " in the *Gentleman's Magazine* for

December, 1788, *Fourteen Sonnets* constituted Bowles's first appearance in print. Not only did Bowles fail to produce anything else so good as the sonnets; he never again attracted the same attention by anything he wrote, except indeed in his various pamphlets against Pope.

About the time he began his work as a poet he also began his work as a clergyman. On May 18, 1788, he was ordained deacon to the curacy of Knoyle (now Bishop's or East Knoyle) in south-west Wiltshire. He took up his residence at a cottage known to-day as " Burlton's " in Donhead St. Mary, a small village near Knoyle and likewise only a few miles from Shaftesbury, where his widowed mother now lived. He was appointed in 1795 to the rectory of Chicklade, and, resigning this, in 1797 to the rectory of Dumbleton; but he never resided at either of these places, nor did the new responsibilities interfere with his duties at Knoyle.

The incumbent at Knoyle was Dr. Charles Wake, who was also a prebendary of Westminster. To his daughter Harriet, Bowles was engaged by 1792. The rector at first looked with favor upon the proposed union; very soon, however, ostensibly because he had heard stories detrimental to Bowles, though more likely because a better match for his daughter seemed obtainable, he violently opposed it. In spite of his opposition, the lovers continued to correspond, and they even met clandestinely a few times after the Wakes went to London for the winter of 1792–93. Through the winter Bowles was buoyed with anticipations of seeing Harriet at Knoyle again in the spring. At the end of March, 1793, however, she was seized with a fever, to which she quickly succumbed. Bowles's bereavement found expression in a number of new pieces which he included in the third edition of his *Sonnets* (1794). In 1797 he married Magdalen Wake, sister of his former *fiancée*. Until her death nearly fifty years later, she remained a most congenial companion and capable helpmate.

During the twenty years following his graduation from Oxford Bowles lived a life of mingled anxiety and achievement. He had inherited a fair amount of property, which he seems to have managed with a good deal of shrewdness. He made visits to London and formed the acquaintance of such men as Sotheby, Sheridan, Beaumont, and Rogers. On the other hand, he did not possess good health, and was several times afflicted with serious illness. Moreover he did not advance professionally as rapidly as he wished. His chief hope of preferment lay in the friendship of Archbishop Moore, who long since had contracted obligations to Bowles's maternal grandfather. Through Bowles's mother an arrangement was made with Moore whereby Bowles was to have the living at Bremhill in north Wiltshire as soon as it became vacant. But the incumbent held on year after year, and meanwhile Bowles saw little of Moore. When the living at last became vacant, the Bishop of Salisbury sent a servant to Bowles to urge that he present himself at Lambeth without an hour's delay. Bowles and his wife set off at once and traveled all night. When they arrived at Lambeth, they found that the archbishop, whose memory was failing, had forgotten his promise and was about to bestow the position upon some other applicant. The repetition of the words "Biddy Grey," the maiden name of Bowles's mother, brought back to Moore a sense of his obligations, and he requested Bowles to wait in London until the arrangements were completed. Bowles waited far beyond the necessary period, then ventured to call upon the archbishop again. He learned that the appointment was his, but that he had failed to notify Moore of his London address.

The collation to the vicarage of Bremhill dates May 22, 1804, though Bowles may not have begun residence until 1805. The promotion came in his forty-second year, and was the turning point in his professional career. The new living brought him, not only an ample salary, but nearly every other advantage he longed for. The vicarage stands on an elevation that looks across the beautiful country around Calne to the Marlborough Downs beyond. The grounds are naturally attractive, and Bowles embellished them with a " lake," a fountain, a stone obelisk, trellis-work arbors, shaded walks, and Shenstonian inscriptions. Some persons, like Moore, felt that he had frittered away the native charm; others were better satisfied. " A perfect paradise of a place," Coleridge called it. It was not so isolated but that London might be visited each year, while Knoyle, Donhead, and Salisbury were within the same county, and Shaftesbury and Bath just over the border. Avebury, Silbury, the Wansdyke, and Stonehenge were near enough for Bowles to gratify the antiquarian taste which Sir Richard C. Hoare, of Stourhead, no doubt did something to foster. Only a few miles distant was Bowood, with its park, its library, its pictures, its gatherings of the notabilities of the kingdom, and (after 1809) its Maecenas-like master, the third Marquis of Lansdowne. Moreover, after the passage of some years Bowles had fairly close neighbors in Crabbe at Trowbridge and Moore at Sloperton Cottage.

In an environment thus pleasant Bowles spent the greater part of his remaining days. He was interested in his parishioners, interested in educating the children of the poor, interested in his choir, and gratified that his congregation increased. The interruptions that came to his quiet life were his annual visits to London, his mingling with the guests at Bowood, his duties on the commission for the peace, his authorship of successive works in prose and verse, and the pamphleteering controversies he waged—on antiquities, on matters

of church and education, on Pope as a man and as
a poet.

Before August, 1828, he was made a canon resident
of Salisbury Cathedral. Thereafter he spent the three
winter months of each year at Salisbury, where perhaps
the most delightful of many agreeable duties were
those in connection with the cathedral music. He
was still much interested in Bremhill, however, and
his return each spring was greeted with joy by his
parishioners.

Though his hearing became increasingly defective,
and his physical powers abated, he displayed marked
energy until he attained his fourth score of years.
From writing he desisted a little earlier. His grief at
the death of his wife (1844) resulted in a state of
almost complete collapse. In January, 1845, he
resigned from his duties at Bremhill, and retired to
Salisbury, where he existed in a state of senile help-
lessness until his death on the 7th of April, 1850. His
death was preceded shortly by that of Wordsworth;
and thus, as he had antedated the great romantic poets,
he likewise survived them.

The personality of Bowles makes a fascinating
study. It contains some qualities which we may
smile at, others which we must regret. To begin with,
he was remarkably simple, naïve, credulous. He
believed that a black man, who had been thrown
overboard from a slaveship, had been found, perfect
and undissolved, in the belly of a porpoise, or, as he
afterwards explained, of a shark. He wore his heart
upon his sleeve: he was delighted with praise of any
sort, and the very first time he met Miss Mitford,
he " talked a great deal of Lord Byron and the Pope
question." In the second place, he was astonishingly
absent-minded. On one occasion when he was dress-
ing for a dinner party, his wife found him in a terrible
" taking " because a silk stocking had unaccountably
disappeared; at length it was learned that he had put

both stockings on one leg. Another time, during a trip on horseback, he dismounted to walk down a steep hill, forgot to remount, and so walked along the turnpike with the reins over his arm until he reached the gate, where his offer to pay toll brought him to his senses and to the discovery that his horse had slipped the bridle and vanished. In the third place, he was one of the greatest cowards, physically, that ever drew breath. " He is literally afraid of everything," wrote Southey. He is said to have measured the distance between his prebendal house and Salisbury Cathedral to ascertain whether he would be in danger if the spire were to fall, and at one time to have " lived in such fear of mad dogs as to wear stout overalls to prevent being bitten." A still more striking instance of his readiness to take affright is recorded at length in a letter (written July 18, 1832) from Caroline Bowles to Southey.

Other qualities are more deplorable. Of these the most prominent are his stubbornness, his combativeness, his extreme conservatism in social, economic, and political affairs, his religious intolerance, and his disposition to impute bad motives to those who advocated principles he disliked.

On the other hand, he was amiable and generous, quickly moved by distress, and fearlessly steadfast on moral issues. He worked hard and unselfishly for the betterment of his community. Though unsophisticated in an extraordinary degree, he showed real acumen in matters of business, and was cultured, and widely talented. He knew and loved music, and was a good if not an accomplished musician. He did not sing or compose well, it is true ; but he played the flute, the violin, and the violoncello, and with all three was probably " a certain though not very rapid performer." Though not an adept in painting, he could " dip the brush " ; he knew moreover where the chief collections were and felt himself competent to pass judgment upon them.   He was an earnest if not a profound student of antiquities.   He was widely acquainted with the best literature.

The most convincing proof of his personal merits is the friendships he made and maintained.   He knew many of the leading personages of his time, and while these men sometimes laughed at him a little, sometimes pitied him, there can be no question that in nearly all cases they genuinely liked him.

II

Bowles's Literary Works

Bowles produced a vast amount of work in prose and verse. Much of it was frankly ephemeral. Of even the more ambitious works only two are remembered, and they but dimly: the *Sonnets* and the criticisms relative to Pope. The irrepealable verdict of mankind has excluded Bowles from the list of great writers. This does not mean, however, that he is without significance. He is one of the transitional writers who bridged the chasm between two centuries and two opposing movements in literature. As such he will always have an interest for scholars. But he deserves far closer attention because he is possibly the most conspicuous example of all time of the lesser poet who has influenced men of consummate genius.

In this place we can make no adequate survey of his literary qualities and productions. We shall do well to confine ourselves to the works that loomed largest in his time, and to a glance at his principal characteristics.

First, his prose. His ambitious efforts in this field came later than his ventures in verse. The earliest of them was an edition of Pope, which he undertook reluctantly and finished in 1806, and which led to a controversy (1819–26) with Campbell, Byron, and others. It is here that we see Bowles as a critic. He does not rank high, yet he had a large share in bringing about the reaction against Pope, and in formulating the literary ideals of his generation.

Of his other prose works the chief are *The Parochial*

History of Bremhill (1828); *Hermes Britannicus,* an antiquarian work (1828); *The Life of Bishop Ken* (2 vols., 1830–31); *Annals and Antiquities of Lacock Abbey* (1835); the autobiographical fragment in *Scenes and Shadows of Days Departed* (1837); and *The Cartoons of Raphael,* a series of sermons (second edition, 1838). All of these have passages of good writing, but as wholes they are neither reliable for their information nor satisfactory for their style, and some of them are decidedly amorphous.

Of the poetry the sonnets were first, but we may reserve them until later. Between 1789 and 1809 Bowles published a large number of short poems, either in separate pamphlets or collectively in volumes. Of these the best is *Coombe Ellen* (1798). *The Sorrows of Switzerland* (1801) is longer and somewhat less impressive. Many of these short poems are imitative; they are saturated, not only with the spirit, but with the very turns of phrase of Milton, Shakespeare, Gray, and others. *The Little Villager's Verse Book,* a volume which gradually grew out of Bowles's wish to connect rural images with moral ideas in verses which might be used in the schools supervised by Mrs. Bowles and the Marchioness of Lansdowne, contains many unpretentious and charming pieces.

In 1804 Bowles expanded an earlier canto on *The Spirit of Navigation* under the new title of *The Spirit of Discovery.* This was the first and least successful of his long poems; more than anything else he wrote perhaps it shows how much he retained of the ideals and methods of the eighteenth century in verse; its purpose is didactic. In 1813 he brought out anonymously a narrative poem, *The Missionary,* which proved the most popular of his longer efforts. In 1822 he ventured again into the narrative field with *The Grave of the Last Saxon,* this time employing blank verse instead of the heroic couplet, and shifting the scene from Chili to England at the time of the Conquest.

In 1828 he published *Banwell Hill*, or *Days Departed*, a poem which traces to some extent his early emotions and experiences somewhat in the manner of *The Prelude*; it contains in one canto a rather effective narrative which he had previously issued under the title of *Ellen Gray*. *St. John in Patmos* (1832) is an unfortunate attempt to make poetic use of Biblical material. On the whole, there can be no doubt that Bowles attained only a measure of even contemporary success in long poems; his nearest approach to triumph was in exotic and romantic narratives inspired by the achievements of Southey and Scott.

This brings us to the *Sonnets*. Bowles tells us he composed them without thought of the strict Italian model, and indeed there is occasionally a slackness in their form which bears out the statement. One of them contains fifteen lines, another opens with a tetrameter, several close with Alexandrines, an many are marred by assonances in contiguous rhyme ies. In considering the rhyme-schemes we should m- ber that the first thirty-two sonnets printed by (n in his edition of the *Poetical Works* were writ y 1797, while none of the remaining fourteen re composed for at least twenty years thereafter. le sonnets of the first group are of a type interm e between the Italian form and that of Surrey; e Surrey in having three quatrains, each with its n set of rhymes; and like the Italian in having e rhymes closed rather than alternate. Thus e standard form consists of three quatrains an t couplet, rhyming *obba cddc effe gg*, and this fo , with some modifications, prevails through the ear group. The effect is not so cumulative as in an Eli bethan sonnet, however, for a slight break or turn the thought is usually discernible at the eighth ninth line, and generally there is no sharply adversati or summarizing emphasis in the concluding couple The sonnets of the second group adhere to the Italia

pattern (*abba abba cdcdcd*), though with slight deviations.

Of the two groups the first contains the better pieces. It is to be remembered that most of these were composed under the stress of a great disappointment—either a broken engagement or a death on the eve of promised marriage. Under circumstances of this kind we should expect from a poet either a proud, Promethean silence or an utterance vibrant with feeling and heightened at times perhaps to momentary frenzy. The incentive was in truth sufficient to lend the sonnets some degree of emotional quality. There are references to "wayward passions that rebel," to crushing bereavements, to the afflictions of struggling mankind; there are glimpses

> "Of rocks amid the sunshine towering dark,
> Of rivers winding wild, or mountains hoar";

but they are fleeting. They are matched by serene pictures from everyday inanimate nature, by placid and at times even conventional phraseology, by eighteenth-century moralizations on Piety and Content. The poet is not mastered by his grief; he toys with it, sentimentalizes it; he sees it in vague retrospection, pensive reminiscence. It is as if we heard subdued music:

> "For when thou leadest all thy soothing strains
> More smooth along, the silent passions meet
> In one suspended transport, sad and sweet;
> And nought but sorrow's softest touch remains;
> That, when the transitory charm is o'er,
> Just wakes a tear, and then is felt no more."

Thus the mood of the sonnets is loitering, languid, sentimental rather than eager, fiery, unquenchable. They are acceptable for their soft atmosphere, their unaffected purity, their graceful melancholy; but they are forgettable, they do not stir us, they leave only an impression of a kind of sad joy in the contemplation

of a happiness that somehow has vanished. Nevertheless from the very fact that they combine the taste and restraint of the old school of poetry with a mild, fragrant freshness of their own, and at the same time avoid the excesses that abortive innovators of poetry were then perpetrating, they were admired and influential in their day, and may be read with pleasure even now. The best of them, though not the most typical structurally, is " The Influence of Time on Grief":

> " O Time! who know'st a lenient hand to lay
> Softest on Sorrow's wound, and slowly thence
> (Lulling to sad repose the weary sense)
> The faint pang stealest unperceived away;
> On thee I rest my only hope at last,
> And think, when thou hast dried the bitter tear
> That flows in vain o'er all my soul held dear,
> I may look back on every sorrow past,
> And meet life's peaceful evening with a smile:—
> As some lone bird, at day's departing hour,
> Sings in the sunbeam, of the transient shower
> Forgetful, though its wings are wet the while:—
> Yet ah! how much must that poor heart endure,
> Which hopes from thee, and thee alone, a cure!"

As has been said, Bowles as a poet is chiefly notable as an influence. He affected Southey, Lamb, and Wordsworth, and the impression he made upon Coleridge is one of the marvels of literature.

III

BOWLES'S RELATIONS WITH HIS CONTEMPORARIES

A. HIS RELATIONS WITH COLERIDGE

IN the latter part of 1789, when Coleridge was a schoolboy at Christ's Hospital, a copy of the second edition of Bowles's *Sonnets* was put into his hands. " My earliest acquaintances," says he, in the opening chapter of *Biographia Literaria*, " will not have forgotten the undisciplined eagerness and impetuous zeal with which I laboured to make proselytes, not only of my companions, but of all with whom I conversed, of whatever rank, and in whatever place. As my school finances did not permit me to purchase copies, I made, within less than a year and a half, more than forty transcriptions, as the best presents I could offer to those who had in any way won my regard. And with almost equal delight did I receive the three or four following publications of the same author."

He adds that he derived two great benefits from his acquaintance with the sonnets during his formative years : (1) they drew him from metaphysics and theological controversy back to poetry, and (2) they drove him, by their difference from the verse then prevalent, to familiarize himself with the principles and the practice of the Greek and the elder English poets, and thus to lay solid foundations for his own literary taste.

His enthusiasm for Bowles continued for some years with but little diminution. He was somewhat disappointed by the alterations he detected in favorite sonnets when the third edition appeared in 1794; but in December of the same year he was regaling

Charles Lamb with recitations from Bowles in " the little smoky room at the ' Salutation and Cat,' " and publishing a sonnet to Bowles in the *Morning Chronicle*. In Pantisocracy days, in early 1795, Bowles was still the god of his idolatry. In the 1796 edition of his own poems he referred to Bowles's superiority as a sonneteer; in the 1797 edition he headed one section " Sonnets, Attempted in the Manner of the Rev. W. L. Bowles "; and in December, 1796, he bound up a miscellany of sonnets with the fourth edition of Bowles, and sent them to Mrs. Thelwall, declaring in a note on the fly-leaf of the Bowles volume: " This volume . . . has given me more pleasure, and done my heart more good, than all the other books I ever read, excepting my Bible."

Early in 1797 Sheridan was looking for a young man of poetical genius to write a tragedy for Drury Lane theatre. Apparently Bowles recommended Coleridge; in any case it was through Bowles that Coleridge was approached. The younger poet, at this time resident at Nether Stowey, entered upon the task with some misgivings. At the end of the first week in September he had finished the tragedy to the middle of Act 5, and set off for Donhead for Bowles's criticism. The first interview between the two men resulted. Coleridge was a guest at Donhead for a week, William Linley, brother-in-law of Sheridan, chancing to be there at the same time. On October 16th Coleridge sent the tragedy (*Osorio*) from Stowey to Donhead. Bowles forwarded it to Sheridan, who rejected but did not return it. In 1813, through the influence of Byron, it was produced, greatly to Coleridge's profit.

After the visit to Donhead Coleridge's friends noticed that he spoke much less frequently about Bowles. He still admired, but not with the old extravagant ardor. His subsequent attitude is concisely indicated in a letter to Sotheby in 1802: " The truth is, Bowles has indeed the *sensibility* of a poet, but he has not the *passion* of a great poet. His later writings all want *native* passion."

From the latter part of 1814 to April, 1816, Coleridge lived with the Morgans at Calne, near Bremhill. Proximity to Bowles, he wrote Rogers in May, 1815, was "a source of constant gratification" to him. It was at this time that he composed *Biographia Literaria*, with its celebrated acknowledgment of his early obligations. At this time also, upon Bowles's recommendation, he applied to Byron for an introduction to a publisher; the result was that such pieces as "Christabel" and "Kubla Khan," though composed long before, were for the first time given to the public. Yet a coolness sprang up between the two men. "Alas!" says Coleridge, "I injured myself irreparably with him by devoting a fortnight to the correction of his poems. He took the corrections, but never forgave the corrector."

From the day Coleridge left Calne the two men moved in almost wholly different spheres. We are not sure they met again. Apart from a complimentary reference or two which Bowles made to Coleridge, we hardly have so much as evidence that they were aware of each other's existence. Upon Coleridge's death Bowles wrote in the *London Times* (August 13, 1834) an account of Coleridge's discharge from the army in 1794. The next year he contributed to the *Gentleman's Magazine* (June, 1835) some details of the visit which Coleridge had paid him at Donhead.

Critics have been disposed to underestimate the influence of Bowles upon the poetry of Coleridge. This upon no better ground than that there *could* not have been much influence. Certainly there is external evidence enough of Coleridge's discipleship until the year 1797. The internal evidence is likewise strong. The very titles of many of the pieces—"lines," "monodies," "Sonnet on Quitting School for College"

—are indicative of the kindred poetic spirit of the younger man. We should expect the surest signs of kinship in the sonnets of Coleridge; and indeed anyone who will compare his " Pain " with Bowles's " The Bells, Ostend," or his " To the River Otter " with Bowles's " To the River Itchin," will admit that the resemblances are marked. But the influence of Bowles is shown, less directly perhaps, though not less clearly, in other pieces written by Coleridge before 1797. How could it be otherwise when he declared in 1796 that " the Sonnets of Bowles . . . domesticate with the heart, and become, as it were, a part of our identity " ? We must not expect that this influence will always be crystallized; it is often held in solution, and requires us to look beyond the words to the mood. What Coleridge admired in Bowles was the tenderness, the naturalness (when Bowles was at his best), the simplicity in thought and expression, the connection of human emotions and moral principles with external scenes, and the soothing, indefinite sentimentality. These qualities did not in all respects affect him for good, but at least they colored a large part of the work that preceded *The Ancient Mariner.* They aroused him to poetry, and were a powerful impulse in much that he wrote until he attained his full poetic stature.

B.   BOWLES'S RELATIONS WITH LAMB

One of the comrades for whom Coleridge transcribed Bowles's *Sonnets* at Christ's Hospital was probably Charles Lamb. Lamb was in the school at that time, and he and Coleridge were friends. Certainly the two men were subsequently in agreement about Bowles, except that Lamb had Cowper and Burns as still greater favorites. He acknowledged, however, that he had " no higher ideas of heaven " than to hear Coleridge reciting " one of Bowles's sweetest sonnets, in your sweetest manner, . . . by

the fire-side at the *Salutation*." He referred, too, to
the nineteenth effusion in Coleridge's volume of 1796
as " that most exquisite and Bowles-like of all ";
declared the description of Mania in Bowles's poem
of " Hope " was " never exceeded "; and asserted:
" Genius of the sacred fountain of tears, it was he
[Bowles] who led you gently by the hand through
all this valley of weeping, showed you the dark green
yew trees and the willow shades where, by the fall of
waters, you might indulge an uncomplaining melancholy, a delicious regret for the past." Furthermore
he admitted that his own beautiful line,

> " To the green plains of pleasant Hertfordshire,"

was copied from Bowles's

> " To the green hamlet on the peaceful plain ";

and he might have added that his sonnets included
in *Poems on Various Subjects* were redolent of Bowles.
After 1797 he makes few or no references to Bowles,
except that in *Mrs. Battle's Opinions on Whist* he states,
perhaps jocosely, that he had sent Bowles the lady's
comments on the game of ombre in Pope, though
they must have reached him " too late to be inserted
among his ingenious notes upon that author." In
1816 Lamb spent a month (the last of July and
probably most of August) at Calne, shortly after
Coleridge's departure from that place. During this
time he was within two miles of Bremhill, but there
is no mention of Bowles in the scant records we have
of this visit. It is possible that the two men never met.

C. BOWLES'S RELATIONS WITH WORDSWORTH

Wordsworth, as a young man, had set out one
morning for a walk from London when a volume of
Bowles's sonnets came somehow into his possession.
He was so delighted with it that he stopped upon one
of the bridges of the Thames and kept his brother

John or else (as another version of the story reports)
several companions waiting while he read the book
through. Nor was the fascination merely momentary.
The *Descriptive Sketches* bear palpable traces of the
influence of Bowles.

This influence, however, was not of very great
duration. The one point at which similarities between
the two men would be looked for is in their sonnets;
yet Wordsworth's first use of this form was inspired
by Milton, and nowhere in it does he seem to have
been affected by the practice of Bowles. Personally
the two poets saw little of each other. On one occasion they were together in a boat on the Thames, but
apparently they were not thrown into each other's
company again until they met in Bath in 1839. This
was probably their last meeting. The most interesting
of the other occasions when we find the two names in
conjunction belongs to the year 1827. Lady Beaumont, hearing that Caroline Bowles " adored " Wordsworth, thought of sending Caroline an invitation to
reside with her. She communicated her idea to
Bowles, however, and he very wisely dissuaded her.

D. BOWLES'S RELATIONS WITH SOUTHEY AND CAROLINE
BOWLES

Southey began his acquaintance with the writings
of Bowles at the age of nineteen, that is, between
August, 1793, and August, 1794. What more likely,
then, that he first heard of them in June of the latter
year, when he first met Coleridge, then on a visit to
Oxford and still captivated by Bowles ? Whoever
introduced him, he was quickly fired with an enthusiasm second only to Coleridge's. At some period
in 1794 he and Robert Lovell called upon Cruttwell,
commended highly the sonnets which had issued from
his press, and desired him to print some poems of
thiers in the same type and form. The volume

appeared in the autumn of that year, though it bears
the imprint " 1795." Some of Southey's pieces,
especially some of his sonnets, show a marked indebtedness to Bowles. Indeed Southey long afterwards said that it was upon Bowles's style that he had
endeavored to model his own.

He was never so completely under the spell as
Coleridge, however, and he was not so slow in throw-
ing it off. We hear of no rhapsodies on his part over
Bowles during the Pantisocracy discussions of 1795.
Before August 26, 1802, he had observed that he,
Coleridge, and Sotheby had too often done themselves
harm by permitting an admiration of Bowles to bubble
up on the surface of their poems. As late as 1807,
nevertheless, he named Bowles among the best
writers of the era; and when he read the anonymous
Missionary in 1814, he praised it with a good deal
of heartiness.

He first saw Bowles in 1802 and, because of
Bowles's unreasonable criticisms of the Welsh bard
Edward Williams, took a dislike to him which was
only dispelled some years afterwards by the repre-
sentations of Sir George Beaumont. By 1815 the two
men had begun a correspondence which lasted, inter-
mittently, as late as 1838. In 1832 their relations
were temporarily strained through Bowles's resentment
of Southey's failure to notice him in reviews. Southey
meanwhile had upheld Bowles in the early stages of
the controversy over Pope, though he probably felt in
the end that his friend had blundered in his conduct
of the argument. Of Bowles's latest work the laureate
did not hold a high opinion. But he was considerate
of Bowles personally, and visited him at Bremhill in
1836. Bowles dedicated a volume of poems, *Scenes
and Shadows of Days Departed* (1837), to Southey,
while the laureate acknowledged his obligations to
Bowles in the preface of his *Poetical Works* (1837).

Possibly Bowles exchanged a letter or two with

Caroline Bowles in the early part of the century; but it was through Southey in 1822 that he became acquainted with her verse. He at once began a correspondence, and claimed kinship with her. In truth they may have been distantly related. He met her in the latter part of 1822 or the earlier part of 1823, and saw her at long intervals during the years that followed. It was she who smoothed out his difficulty with Southey in 1832. Her correspondence with Southey, which has been edited by Professor Dowden, contains many illuminating references to him.

E. BOWLES'S RELATIONS WITH CRABBE AND MOORE

Crabbe was inducted into the living at Trowbridge in June, 1814. On February 9, 1815, he met Bowles, apparently for the first time, at a dinner at Colonel Houlton's at Farleigh Castle. We know that Bowles rode over to Trowbridge with Lord Lansdowne to call on Crabbe, but this was probably after a winter season during which Lansdowne was in London and Bowles had cultivated Crabbe's acquaintance.

It seems to have been through Bowles that Crabbe met, not only Lansdowne, but later both Moore and Rogers. Trowbridge was not close enough to Bremhill for anything like constant intercourse, but each poet knew that after all the other was within reach. Though in a literary way neither had much effect upon the other (they were too old for that), they agreed in public and private matters: Crabbe staunchly supported Bowles in the Catherine Cook case, and the kindliness of their personal relations was fittingly commemorated when the younger Crabbe dedicated to Bowles his biography of his father.

Moore came to Sloperton Cottage in 1817. He had probably met Bowles before, but now began an intercourse which lasted through practically the rest of Bowles's life. Sloperton was within walking distance of Bremhill, and both men were frequent guests at

Bowood. Bowles's carriage was always at Moore's disposal; so were Bowles's social qualities. Moore did not think highly of the literary gifts of his neighbor, and was sometimes amused at his personal oddities; but their relations were throughout of a nature thoroughly cordial. Moore's *Diary* is one of the richeſt sources of our knowledge of Bowles.

F. BOWLES'S RELATIONS WITH SHERIDAN AND ROGERS

It was at a boating party " on Hampton's waters " that Bowles firſt met Sheridan. The date of the meeting is not known; but as Sheridan in 1795 made the daughter of Dr. Newton Ogle, Dean of Wincheſter, his second wife, and as Bowles was not only acquainted with Ogle, but along with Mrs. Sheridan was subsequently a gueſt of Ogle's son at a water-party on the Beaulieu River, it seems likely that Ogle was the man who introduced them. In that case, the meeting probably took place after 1792, when the firſt Mrs. Sheridan died. However that may be, Bowles attended one of Sheridan's morning concerts and there met Sheridan's brother-in-law, Linley, in 1796. In 1797 he procured the submission of *Osorio* to Drury Lane. Seven years later he employed Sheridan in securing permission to dedicate his *Spirit of Discovery* to the Prince of Wales. After Sheridan's death, he commemorated in verse the social and personal merits of his friend.

When Bowles met Rogers we do not know. Probably it was during one of his visits from Donhead to London. About the end of the century a liſt of gueſts at one of Rogers's breakfast parties included his name. Thereafter it is certain that he was often received at Rogers's house, and that Rogers executed various minor commissions for him when he could not come to the city. Some years later Rogers was in turn being entertained at Bowood and Bremhill. It was the banker-poet who suggested to Bowles that he write a narrative in verse, and Rogers was irritated when the second edition of *The Missionary* was dedicated to Lansdowne instead of himself.   Nevertheless he took up Campbell sharply on the day of Byron's funeral for speaking of Bowles as a rascal.   The two men maintained their intercourse as late as 1839, probably still later.

G.   BOWLES'S RELATIONS WITH THE LANSDOWNES

Lord Shelburne, the first Marquis of Lansdowne, was an early host of Bowles at Southampton Castle. The second Marquis seems also to have befriended him.   But when the third was established at Bowood (1809), Bowles found himself blessed with amenities which surpassed the advantages of old-time literary patronage and offered none of its drawbacks.   Lansdowne was one of the most conspicuous and upright of English statesmen during the first half of the century.   He was also a lover of the fine arts, while with the aid of the Marchioness he made Bowood a social capital of England.   Under his roof Bowles met many of the notabilities of Europe; and through him such persons as Dugald Stewart, Sir Humphrey Davy, Madame de Staël, and in 1837 the Prime Minister and the Secretary of State, were brought to Bremhill.   Well might Bowles say that at his vicarage he had " had far greater advantage than worldly wealth, the inestimable advantage of the friendly and social intercourse for so many years, with such a family as that at Bowood."   Mrs. Bowles was an indispensable auxiliary to Lady Lansdowne in practical undertakings and charitable enterprises.   It will be seen that most of the correspondence between the two families belongs to the winter seasons when the Lansdownes were in the metropolis.

H. BOWLES'S RELATIONS WITH BYRON

In the first edition of *English Bards and Scotch Reviewers*, which was issued in March, 1809, was a satirical passage on Bowles. It was really from the pen of Hobhouse. In the second edition, which appeared in October, Byron substituted a passage of his own, in which he berated Bowles for the edition of Pope, ridiculed the *Sonnets*, and indulged in gibes at the expense of *The Spirit of Discovery*, particularly at the episode, in the fourth book, of the two lovers kissing on the island of Madeira. Three years later Bowles's called the nobleman's attention to a misrepresentation of the Madeira episode, probably caused by acquaintance with a distorted version of it in the *Edinburgh Review*; and Byron admitted the justice of the charge. The two men met several times in London drawing-rooms; and Byron, though amused at " the pastoral innocence " of Bowles's conversation, admitted that he told good stories, and was " a pleasant, gentlemanly man—a good fellow, for a parson." Through Murray, Bowles brought to Byron's notice some letters of the nobleman's ancestor; and when Coleridge, prompted by Bowles, applied to Byron for his influence in finding a publisher, Byron sent his " best respects to Mr. Bowles." Zealous admiration of Pope, and love of mischief, induced Byron to enter the controversy which Campbell had precipitated, but Bowles's somewhat insinuating courtesy caused him to withdraw from it. Though he had scant respect for Bowles as a literary man, and thought of him as " fussily fishing on for fame," he paid tribute to the merits of *The Missionary*.

I. MISCELLANEOUS CONNECTIONS

Bowles maintained cordial relations with several of his publishers, notably Cruttwell, Cadell and Davies, Nichols, Murray, and Pickering. He maintained long friendships with John Wilson (" Christopher North "), Beaumont, Sotheby, Alaric Watts, John Mitford, and others. He knew Sir Walter Scott, though not intimately. He had some acquaintance with Madame de Staël, Barry Cornwall, Landor, Lockhart, and John Scott, but alienated Scott by indiscreetly using his name in connection with the controversy over Pope. He seems not to have met De Quincey ; nor Hazlitt, who contemptuously gave him the palm in the discussion with Byron ; nor Keats, whom he would probably have branded as a Cockney ; nor Shelley, whose atheism would have repelled him. Shelley, however, seems to have had a share in deterring Byron from publishing his second letter on Pope ; and it was at the summer residence in Radnorshire of a favorite cousin of Shelley (Thomas Grove) that Bowles wrote *Coombe Ellen*. Of the periodicals, *The Gentleman's Magazine* and *Blackwood's* were invariably friendly to Bowles, while the *Quarterly* and *Edinburgh Reviews* were harshly hostile.

LETTERS

Coleridge to Bowles

NETHER STOWEY,
March (?), 1797.[1]

Dear Sir,

But that I am not likely to have another opportunity of transmitting the accompanying trifles[2] to you, I would not intrude on you at a moment, when your heart is necessarily occupied with its own feelings. You have the nightly prayers of my little family for the restoration of your dear Mother's health. To me the death of the aged has a more mournful effect than that of the young. Accustomed to observe a completeness in all the works of Nature, the departure of the latter seems more of a *transition*—the heart is dissatisfied and says, *This cannot be all.* But of the aged we have seen the bud, the blossom, and the fruit, and the whole circle of existence appears completed. But praise and thanksgiving to Him who sent light and immortality into the world, bidding the corruptible put on incorruption, and the mortal immortality: for the young and old alike rejoice before God and the Lamb.

The poems of Mr. Lloyd will, I think, please you. The woman, whom they lament,[3] approached as near perfection as human nature admits. This affection

[1] The letter could not have been written much earlier than March, 1797, as Coleridge did not contemplate a tragedy until about that time. The death of Bowles's mother on March 25, 1797, sets the latest limit.

[2] Perhaps an advance copy of the second edition of his *Poems,* which was published the following July. It included pieces by Charles Lamb and Charles Lloyd.

[3] Lloyd's grandmother, Priscilla Farmer.

for her was almost too great, for her death has had
the most melancholy effects on his health—he fell into
a nervous complaint, which has terminated in a species
of epileptic seizures. He is at present domesticated
in my cottage.[1] My Ode[2] you will read with a friendly
forbearance as to its political sentiments. The base
of our politics is, I doubt not, the same. We both
feel strongly for whomever our imaginations present
to us in the attitude of suffering. I confess, that mine
is too often a " *stormy* pity."

The plan I have sketched for my tragedy is too
chaotic to be transmitted at present—but immediately
I understand it myself, I will submit it to you: and
feel greatly obliged to you for your permission to do
it. It is " romantic and wild and somewhat terrible "
—and I shall have Siddons and Kemble[3] in my mind.
But indeed I am almost weary of the terrible, having
been an hireling in the Critical Review for these last
six or eight months. I have been lately reviewing the
Monk, the Italian, Hubert de Sevrac,[4] &c., &c., in
all of which dungeons, and old castles, and solitary
Houses by the Sea Side, and Caverns, and Woods, and
extraordinary characters, and all the tribe of Horror
and Mystery, have crowded on me—even to surfeiting.

I rejoice to hear of your new edition.[5] Why did
you ever omit that sublime Sonnet, Thou, whose stern

---

[1] Lloyd had taken up residence with Coleridge in September, 1796.
[2] The " Ode on the Departing Year " is the opening poem of the
volume.
[3] Sarah Siddons (1755–1831) and her brother John Philip Kemble
(1757–1823), then the leading tragedians of the English stage.
[4] The reviews are reprinted in another section of this volume.
[5] Probably the sixth (1798), which contains 30 sonnets and 16
other pieces. The first (1789) contains 14 sonnets, the second (1789)
21 sonnets, the third (1794) 27 sonnets and 13 pieces, the fourth (1796)
the same, the fifth (1796) 27 sonnets and 15 pieces. If we make a
few textual corrections which the poet calls for at the end of the third
edition, the sonnets of this edition are in precise agreement with those
of the fourth and fifth. Which of the three Coleridge possessed at this
time I cannot say.

Spirit loves the awful ſtorm—?[1] I should have pleaded hard too for the firſt, Bereave me not[2]—and ſtill more vehemently for the Sonnet to Harmony,[3] the only description of the effeçt of Music that suited my experience, or rose above common place. [In Sonn]et XVI (as they now stand) the parenthesis always [interr]upts the tide of my feelings.[4] We describe [beſt for o-(?)] -thers not when we speak *to* the objeçt described. Perhaps I may be wrong, but I am sure, you will excuse my freedom. I do not like your alterations of Evening[5]—it seems now to possess less *oneness* than it did before. In the 18th[6] you use " hope " in two ways, once as an abſtraçt—he with new hope—once as an impersonation—Sweet Hope! Is this an imperfeçtion ? I could write a great deal about your late alterations, but I will not detain you any more.

Believe me,
Very sincerely yours,
S. T. COLERIDGE.

Thursday Morning.
I shall be anxious to learn of your dear Parent's Health.

---

[1] The 31st in Gilfillan's 2-volume edition of Bowles's *Poetical Works* (1855). After appearing in the second edition, it had been omitted from the three following ones. It was not inserted in the sixth.

[2] The 30th in Gilfillan. It had been in the second edition ; Bowles did not reprint it in the sixth.

[3] The 28th in Gilfillan. In the second ; reprinted in the sixth.

[4] The 17th in Gilfillan. In the sixth edition Bowles removed an awkward parenthesis which had marred lines 2–4 in all previous editions.—(The last paragraph of the letter is badly torn in several places.)

[5] Sonnet 6 in Gilfillan. Coleridge's criticism is somewhat captious, and Bowles did not adopt it fully in the sixth edition.

[6] The 18th in Gilfillan. It had first appeared in the third edition. Coleridge's criticism is sound, and Bowles heeded it in the sixth edition.

Coleridge to Bowles

STOWEY, near BRIDGEWATER,
Monday, Oct. 16*th,* 1797.

My dear Sir

At laſt I send you the Tragedy complete and neatly transcribed. I have sent another to Mr. Linley. I have endeavoured to strike out the charaƈter of Warville, the Englishman;[1] and to subſtitute some more intereſting one—but in vain. So I have altered his name, made him a German, and a nothing at all. Perhaps I had better have given Albert a *confidential servant*—*he* might have cleaned Albert's shoes, &c— whereas what Maurice does or *can* do, is not quite so clear. In truth, I have lagged so long at the work, and see so many imperfeƈtions in the original and main plot, that I feel an indescribable disguſt, a sickness of the very heart, at the mention of the Tragedy. If there be any thing with which I am at all satisfied, it is—the style. I have endeavoured to have few sentences which *might not* be spoken in conversation, avoiding those that are *commonly* used in conversation.[2] —You, I know, will forward it to Mr. Sheridan with all speed; and will be so kind as to write to him on the subjeƈt.—Excepting for the money which would be gained if it succeeded, I am not conscious of a wish relating to the piece. It is done: and I would

---

[1] It has been known (see E. H. Coleridge : *Complete Poetical Works of S. T. Coleridge*, Vol. II, pp. 580–81) that " Warville " may have been an earlier name for the attendant of Osorio's brother Albert ; but Coleridge here adds to our knowledge of the evolution of the character. Possibly Bowles, in September, had advised some sort of change.

[2] A succinct and luminous statement of Coleridge's theory of the poetic use of everyday language. It is all the more interesting because it shows that Coleridge had matured his thought on this subject before Wordsworth's famous and more extreme utterance upon it.

rather mend hedges and follow the plough, than write another. I could not avoid attaching a pecuniary importance to the business; and consequently, became anxious: and such anxieties humble and degrade the mind.

I hope you are well. Give my respects to Mrs. Bowles, and believe me, with great sincerity,

Your obliged,

S. T. COLERIDGE.

P.S.—I should very much wish to see your Spirit and Progress of Discovery[1] before it is printed. You might be sure, that I would shew it to no human being, except my wife.

You will be so kind as with the Tragedy to transmit this little volume[2] to Mr. Sheridan.

[1] Published in incomplete form as *The Spirit of Navigation and Discovery*, and later (1804) in complete form as *The Spirit of Discovery*.

[2] Perhaps the 1797 edition of Coleridge's *Poems*. At an earlier date Coleridge had sent his sonnet to Sheridan to that dramatist through Bowles.

D

Bowles to Wordsworth

BREMHILL, near CHIPPENHAM,
April ye 15*th,* [1839].

My dear Mr. Wordsworth[1]

Connected by so many and affecting reminiscences, and so much of more higher reason for
veneration, it would have been of great satisfaction
and gratification if you could have look'd on me in
my old parsonage domain. You will find the Fishers,
and their wonderful child,[2] and I shall tru[ly] regret
not being there. But I shall come to Bath, and shake
you by the hand, not having seen you, I think, since
you and I, and Rogers, were in a boat together, on
the *Thames,* and I *got out* and *run away,* and I heard
you pronounc'd—My, the *boldest man* in England ![3]

Whether this be true or not, I shall face all dangers
of *two post* horses to come and see you *Thursday* next,
at *one* o'clock.

[1] The letter is addressed to Wordsworth at 10 George St., Bath.
[2] William Fisher, Canon of Salisbury, had married Wordsworth's
first cousin, Elizabeth Cookson. Their daughter, Emmeline, was a
child-poet of extraordinary gifts. She was much admired by Wordsworth and other good judges.
[3] Rogers tells the story thus : " Wordsworth, Mrs. Wordsworth,
their daughter, and Bowles, went upon the Thames in a boat, one fine
summer's day. Though the water was as smooth as glass, Bowles very
soon became so alarmed, that he insisted on being set ashore ; upon
which Wordsworth said to him, ' Your confessing your cowardice is
the most striking instance of valor that I ever met with.' " (Powers :
Samuel Rogers, p. 200).

I am much alter'd in phiz., but not, I hope, much either in heart or head, at least I persuade myself so; but with respect and regard for you, privately and publickly, I am sure not; and believe me

Ever, &c.,

W. L. BOWLES.

Do not write, if Thursday will suit you. Southey is with my *namesake*, Caroline—and I hope, and believe, the attachment will lead to happiness the most enviable in this life, and who but must wish so, who ever read Southey's exquisite Hymn *to the Penates !*

I am truly glad to find your *outward machine* is only a little worse for *wear !* I am as *Wizen* as a *Witch*, and as *Deaf* as a *Post !*

Bowles to Wordsworth

BREMHILL,

April 22, [1839].

My dear Mr. Wordsworth,[1]

I should have written to you sooner to thank you and Mrs. Wordsworth for your *more* than *kind* welcome, but I wished to hear first from the oldest friend I have[2] and whose unrivaled pictures I mention'd to you.

I hope by this time you have seen him and them ! I mention'd to their owner the interesting anecdote which you told me, and I trust the sight of pictures, landscapes and portraits so beautiful upon earth will inspirit you not to let the design slumber !

To-day I have been over to Moore's and told him

---

[1] Letter directed to Bath.

[2] Perhaps Lord Arundell of Wardour. When at Donhead, Bowles had been his neighbor and enjoyed his hospitality. *The Parochial History of Bremhill* was dedicated to him. Had Lansdowne's pictures been the ones Wordsworth was to see, Bowles should not have been uncertain whether the inspection had taken place.

that I went to Bath on purpose to see you, and how glad I was to find you so well.

He is anxious to see you, and was easily persuaded to come over to a morning's concert on Friday ! He, Mrs. Moore and young Tom come in my carriage, and he and myself mean to call on you and Mrs. Wordsworth, about one o'clock, before the concert, and with the kindest, believe me, ever, my dear Mr. Wordsworth——[1]

If our calling on you at that time should be in the slightest manner inconvenient write a line to me at the White Hart, and how rejoiced I should feel if you would partake of our fare, at the inn, for I have order'd the very same fare as that with which you treated us so sumptuously, and we shall sit down as soon as the concert is over, and get back in the evening.

Mrs. Bowles desires to send her best remembrances, hoping you have heard a good account from your son.

Ever truly and affectionately,

W. L. BOWLES.

---

[1] The disjointedness of the two letters to Wordsworth is probably due to Bowles's absent-mindedness and old age.

Southey to Rev. C. T. Latrobe

15 QUEEN ANNE ST.,
CAVENDISH SQ.,
3 *June*, 1820.

Sir[1]

It is a matter of surprise to me, as well as of concern, that the Moravians should feel themselves aggrieved by any part of the history of Mr. Wesley's life. With that subject the history of the U. Brethren is intimately connected; to describe them therefore, such as they were at that time, was a necessary part of the task which I had undertaken. I spoke of the extravagances, into which they had run, and the dangers from which they had escaped, not in malice, neither, as you seem to imply, from the mere desire of amusing my readers by enlivening the subject, but as a matter of history, which it was my business, in the strict line of duty, to notice, for example and instruction. And whether this was done with an unfriendly or uncharitable spirit, I may leave, sir, to your own decision. It is distinctly stated, that the early Moravians were innocent of the crimes which were laid to their charge, that they saw the errors which they had committed, and that they corrected

---

[1] Southey's *Life of Wesley* was published in two volumes in 1820. The Rev. C. T. Latrobe, a Moravian, objected in a letter to Southey on May 27, 1820, to passages regarding certain hymns and fanaticisms of the early Moravians. He was dissatisfied with Southey's reply and on June 5th forwarded it to Bowles, saying : " I owe [this] to your kindness, in endeavouring to do away the unpleasant impressions made upon my mind, (which, however, I am sorry to say, are very general among those of our Church, who have read the work)."

them.   It is said, in explicit condemnation of Mr. Wesley, that in no other incident of his life did he act so disingenuously, as when he repeated and accredited the calumnies against them, and it is directly affirmed, that, at this day, they enjoy the general good opinion of every other religious community.   As the biographer of Mr. Wesley, I expected to be assailed from many quarters, but certainly not from the Moravians.

.   .   .   .

Nothing could be farther from my thoughts and intentions than to give offence to the Moravians, or to impute to them any participation in the fanatical and perilous language of their predecessors.   But as the present body are no ways answerable for their errors, so I must be allowed to maintain, that their meritorious conduct cannot be pleaded as a reason, why in an historical account of the Society, all mention of such errors should be suppressed.   This would be surely as unreasonable, as it would be in a history of the Church of England to omit the crimes of Henry 8th and other actions, by which our blessed Reformation was sullied.

The notes, of which you complain, were added as proofs of what had been asserted in the text, and as the page to which they relate is referred to, I should have thought it never could have been supposed that any injury was done, or intended to the existing Society.   Nevertheless, that this may be entirely understood, I will in any future edition alter the superscription of those extracts as you suggest.   And if you wish that a distinct disavowal on my part of any injurious intention toward the Moravians should be laid before the public, you have my consent to publish this letter in any manner you may think proper.   I remain, sir, with great personal respect,

Yours obediently,

ROBERT SOUTHEY.

To Rev. C. T. Latrobe.

Caroline Bowles to Bowles

BUCKLAND, 1*st August*, 1822.[1]

I hope you will *not* find " The Widow's Tale " at Bremhill, at least any other copy of it than that which I request you will do me the favor to accept. The poor little book (which would have been faulty enough even in a *perfect* state) is full of misprints and blunders, one of which only concerns me much however. It is the false orthography of " ign*es* fatui." I had written the words *right*, *by chance*, (as a parrot echoes what he has been used to hear) for I am in truth as ignorant and uneducated a scribbler as ever spoiled innocent paper, but afterwards, mistrusting my own *learning*, I asked of one who *should* have known better, " Is that right ? "—" Oh, no," said he, for it was a he, " you should have written it ign*i* fatui," and so I did sans plus, and the printer has been perversely exact in recording the blunder.

It is very absurd perhaps to trouble you with all this " much ado about nothing." I know it savours of egregious egotism, but I confess myself ambitious of your good opinion, and I would much rather have the charge of writing bad poetry brought against me than that of presumptuous ignorance, affecting *fine*

---

[1] Caroline Bowles's first two published works were *Ellen Fitz-arthur* (1820) and *The Widow's Tale, and Other Poems* (1822). On July 7, 1822, Southey writes Caroline that he has asked Bowles whether he had read the two poems, and has learned that he had trumpeted the first to the Lansdownes " and all the *literati*," and will now look for the second. Also he says Bowles speaks of writing her a note and sending her his poem (presumably *The Grave of the Last Saxon*). On July 17th Caroline tells Southey that she is thanking Bowles by that day's post for his gift. She says playfully, further, that she is charging him with neglecting her as a kinswoman when, years before, she claimed relationship with the writer of the *Sonnets*,

diction, and *fine* words. If ever I meddle with the dead languages again ! may I be restricted like Fatima from the use of my mother tongue.

I thank you heartily for your good word, for the kind words I know you have spoken to many, of my first venture. Time was when such encouragement might have spurred me on, inspired me to the attempt at least, of something better, but now " the evil days " seem come upon me, and the " silver string so loosened " that there is no elasticity of spirit left. Enough however to wish for the pleasure of becoming personally acquainted with you, and if my health mends I *may* be in your neighbourhood about the latter end of September or the beginning of October. Till then I shall be at home, or within call from home at least, and most happy to see you should you " wander this way." I will even venture on the ground of our *relationship* (no longer debateable land) to add that you would find a bed for yourself and shelter for your horse at my little dwelling—very homely accommodations in truth, but as comfortable as good will could make them.

.   .   .   .

I will give your message to Mr. Southey. The dispraise of *some* is full as honourable to him as the high respect and admiration in which he is held by others.[1] Dogs bay at the moon.

Believe me,
Very truly yrs.,
CAROLINE A. BOWLES.

---

[1] Various recriminations were passing at this time between Southey and Byron in connection with Southey's *Vision of Judgment* (1821). The reference is probably to some of these.

Caroline Bowles to Bowles

WOODBINE COTTAGE,
LEAMINGTON, WARWICKSHIRE,
July 5th, 1823.

My dear Sir

In my way thro' Oxford about a week ago, I heard of you from two different persons (Mr. Duncan and Mr. Allen) and both told me it was your intention to favour me with a visit at Buckland some time after the Salisbury assizes. I should have received this intimation with real pleasure, had I been travelling *home*wards, instead of *on*wards to this place, and ultimately (if I am so fortunate as to regain a little health and strength here) to Derbyshire and the Lakes.

Lady Bumond (who had the pleasure of being introduced to you in town) had mentioned to me your kind intention, and that she had apprised you of my probable absence from home. She told me besides that you proposed writing to me, and even hinted at some possibility that you might yourself visit the Lakes this autumn.

I fear however she was mistaken in her communications, both so agreeable to me, and I feel so reluctant that you should visit my little dwelling during the absence of its mistress, and so desirous of reserving for myself at some future day (if indeed I may talk of the future ?) the pleasure of receiving you there, that I venture to intrude on you now the unimportant communication of my present place of sojourn and my scheme of further progress. The latter is as yet only sketched out, but if reviving health and hope enable me to fill up the now faint outline, I shall probably be at Keswick somewhere about the middle of August, till which time Mr. Southey will be absent from thence, and I would not approach the land of song while the habitation of the mighty minstrel is vacant.

Was you ever at this place ? It is very beautiful,

and the neighbourhood so rich in objects of interest, that I long for a little strength to visit and enjoy them, and wish I could conjure hither my little carriage and New Forest poney.

Every body here says to me, " Oh ! don't take the trouble of going to Stratford upon Avon. We have been, and there is *nothing* to see, absolutely nothing. An ugly place, just the walls of an old mean house that they call Shakespeare's, and his tomb in the Church. Don't go." I listen in silence, but my heart burns within me to visit those very " nothings " I am cautioned against. And Kenilworth is become classic ground ! I only want somebody to enjoy these things with me, but the people here think of nothing but balls, and lotteries, and dress. I hope the one day I spent in your company at Mr. Wiltcline's will not be the last of our meeting.

Believe me, my dear sir,
Very truly yrs.,
CAR. A. BOWLES.

Bowles to Caroline Bowles

BREMHILL, *November 9th*, 1823.

My dear Madam :

As Mr. Southey is coming to the South, pray, make known to him my anxious hope that I shall see him here, and perhaps you would accompany him, tho I am rather loth you should see Bremhill in this desolating and desolate season.

As to the Doctor, I did not mean to deceive you, for I thought as Caroline did not write the Poem,[1] she would think from what I said another Bowles might. The sole reason of my putting another name was the petty malice of some of those votaries of " Apollar," in a certain kingdom of Cokaine, whom

---

[1] *Ellen Gray.* Bowles had published it, under the pseudonym " Dr. Archibald McLeod," earlier in the year. Its preface contains sharp reflections upon the literary taste then prevalent.

I was willing to deceive as I had once done before, but surely there is not much " treachery " in doing that by which no human being is injured and by which I might escape gross insult, for my preface would be considered as an attack on the admirers of false simplicity, false sentiment, and false sublimity !

Why was not Caroline Bowles' name put to the beautiful verses, on Sunday Evening, instead of that little letter, C. ? I am, however, too well acquainted with a style so delightful, to be deceived.

I am glad you had so pleasant a journey " to the Land of Song." " The writah," as you call him, engaged to come here some hours ago, but neither came or sent an excuse ! Moore was here some few days ago, and was in singing indeed, come un ange ! but I always set him to Purcel-Mozart, Haydn, having no great relish for much of his own music. With expression the most exquisite, he seems to want the idea of what is most sublime or pathetic, in music or poetry—but in the last he can be most beautiful, as witness some of his purer lyrics, and the Peri at all events. He is an example, in private life, of domestic happiness, and irreproachable conduct.

I met yesterday, at Methuen's of Corsham, an acquaintance of yours who spoke of you with much regard, W'm Rose, but his wit, when he condescended to talk, is too elaborate for me. Lord Lansdowne is in Paris; otherwise I would have sent a frank, and I was willing not to lose any time, fearing Southey might have left you.

My old friend, the Bishop of London and his family, passed a couple of days here, a few days ago, but there is no one in [the] world whom I should be more happy to see than Mr. Southey, of whom I have a far higher opinion than of any writer of the age.

Believe me to be, dear madam,

Always most truly,

W. L. BOWLES.

Southey to Bowles

KESWICK, 19 *March*, 1825.

My dear Sir

I am induced to write to you by a letter which I have this day received from G. Peachy.[1]   In answer to the request which he communicates, though I am little behind you in the vale of years,—and likely perhaps to reach the end of our mortal journey by a shorter road,—yet, should I prove the survivor, any wish which you may please to signify, I will faithfully, and to the best of my power, discharge.   There are three contemporaries the influence of whose poetry on my own I can distinctly trace: Sayers, yourself, and Walter Landor.   I owe you something therefore on the score of gratitude.

But to a pleasenter subject.   Peachy tells me that you had begun to print some observations upon Mr. Butler's book,[2] but that you have supprest them upon hearing that I was engaged in answering it.   I am sorry for this, because the more answers that are called forth, the better.   False and shallow as the book is, (the Bishop of London calls it very justly " a flimsy structure of misstatements and sophistry,") it imposes upon the re- [blot on MS.] and is gladly appealed to as an authority by the Liberals who are this time leagued against the church. . . . The church ought not to be without defenders at this time.

---

[1] General Peachey, of Bath, was one of Southey's correspondents, hence a good medium for Bowles's request that Southey should, at least in some degree, act as his executor.   Peachey's first wife, Emma Frances Charter Peachey, had died at Madeira in 1809, and Bowles had written elegiac verses upon her.   Her sister, Elizabeth Charter, was admired by Southey and half loved by Crabbe.

[2] Southey's pleasingly written but superficial and prejudiced *Book of the Church* (1824) had been answered by Charles Butler.   Thereupon Southey published his *Vindiciæ Anglicanæ* in 1826.

If the Catholic writers had been put down whenever they appeared during the last five and twenty years, as they might and ought to have been, by an exposure of their gross and impudent misrepresentations, their party would not be so daring as it now is.

Dr. Phillpotts is answering the theological part of Butler's book. My business of course must be to attack him along the whole of his line,—which I am doing most effectually. For the sake of relieving the tone of controversy I take the opportunity of introducing biographical and historical matter, and call my work therefore *Vindiciæ Ecclesiæ Anglicanæ : The Book of the Church*, vindicated and amplified. My temper is not controversial. I had much rather be industriously and thankfully reading old books, than detecting the defects and vices of new ones. But when I am provoked to it, I can wield a sledge hammer to as good purpose as my old friend Wat Tyler himself.[1]

You will have seen in the last *Quarterly Review* a paper of mine upon Hayley. Gifford did not like its temper, and while the *Review*, owing to his state of health was under a Regency composed of I know not who,[2] I believe the paper would have been kicked out without ceremony,—if it had been quite convenient to kick out the author with it. They frightened Murray about it, till he was persuaded that it would do great disservice both to literature and morals,—and wrote to tell me so. I answered this communication at some length, and in a tone which I think must have made the Regents somewhat ashamed. Murray, which is much to his credit, put my letter into the hands of the new editor,—and the

---

[1] In 1794 Southey wrote a drama *Wat Tyler*, which was full of republican sentiment. It was issued for the first time, and piratically, in 1817, long after Southey's opinions had changed.

[2] Gifford resigned from the editorship of the *Quarterly Review* in 1824. John Taylor Coleridge succeeded him. Lockhart became editor in 1825.

poor paper which had been postponed for two numbers then made its appearance. The two sentences which convey the most decided censure I inserted in the proofs eight months ago to satisfy Gifford,—which of course I would not have done, if the censure had not been perfectly just. But from my heart I abhor that sort of criticism which serves only to gratify an acrimonious spirit in the writer, and to excite or cherish one in the reader.

I hear often from your cousin Caroline, who holds a very high place in my esteem. She sent me a pen and ink drawing the other day which I would not exchange for Sir George Beaumont's Claude (?)[1]: it was a portrait of herself, her poor old nurse, and her dog, with a sweet, sad poem annexed to it.

God bless you, my dear sir.

Yrs. very truly,
ROBERT SOUTHEY.

Caroline Bowles to Bowles

BUCKLAND, 8*th Decr.*, 1827.

At last, my dear sir, I send you the little sketches I promised to attempt as illustrations of your beautiful Hymn Book.[2] It deserves a better illustrator, but you must take the will for the deed. This morning while sorting some papers, the enclosed reappeared from among the rubbish. It was written on my birthday[3]—*this day* ten years. *That* was the *first*

---

[1] Sir George Beaumont gave his collection of pictures to promote the formation of a national gallery, an object dear to his heart. To a Claude (now number 61 in the National Gallery) he was so attached, however, that he requested to have it returned to him for his lifetime.

[2] Presumably *The Village Verse Book* (later called *The Little Villager's Verse Book*). The fourth edition appeared in 1827.

[3] She was born October 7, 1786.

birthday to which I had opened my eyes unawakened by some beloved voice, and I was still young enough then to feel the desolation acutely.   The day was Sunday—a Communion Sunday, and I found peace and consolation at the altar.   Under such circumstances the accompanying lines were composed, or rather my feelings so fashioned themselves into verse. I never showed or gave the little sonnet for publication. It was not for indifferent eyes—but yours are not such, and however your taste may criticise the verse, you will fully enter into the feeling it attempts to express.

Do you know you left a pledge—not a defiance, I hope—when you *appeared* to me last summer for that brief moment.[1]   You left a pair of gloves, and tho' I will not stick them in my bonnet, I will keep them till you come to redeem the token.

Meanwhile, my dear sir,

And believe me ever,

Most truly yours,

CAROLINE A. BOWLES.

Bowles to Caroline Bowles

BREMHILL, *March 1st*, 1828.

My dear Madam

I shall have great pleasure in sending you my plain statement of all the circumstances of the case of the poor woman whom I was able to deliver from her horrible doom;[2] but my warm friends, Lord

---

[1] Bowles had made her a short visit July 2, 1827.

[2] Bowles had obtained a mitigation in the sentence of Catherine Cook, upon whom heavy judgment had been passed for a comparatively slight offence.   This angered some of his brother-magistrates, and at Devizes on January 15, 1828, they passed a vote of censure against him, though Crabbe, Benett, and others opposed it vigorously. The incident aroused much excitement in the county, which sided with Bowles.

Radnor, Wm. Benett, the member for the county,[1] all have found me hard and fast, thinking the effort against me too absurd to deserve notice, and anxious for the sake of the peace of the county, that nothing more should be said.   I beg to return my warmest thanks for the interest you and Lady Neale (?) have taken in the subject, and believe me always

Most truly, &c.,

W. L. BOWLES.

I saw " our George " at Bath[2] the other day.   Pray, remember me to Sir Harry, when you see him, and my old friend George Bumond (?)

Bowles to Caroline Bowles

[BREMHILL], 16th May, [1829].

My dear Madam

I trouble you again because a letter has been sent here, directed to Miss C. Bowles, which I have forwarded to you, supposing it directed here by mistake; and because I would not appear ungrateful to you after having receiv'd so kind and heart-felt a letter.   It is indeed most gratifying to me to receive such a testimony[3] from a mistress of genuine pathos and delightful imagery.   I am almost afraid to say what I feel, lest I should be thought to deal in that sort of language which poetical elderly gentlemen sometimes address to ladies of literature, but I assure you I set the highest value on the opinions of a lady

---

[1] I think John Benett of Pyt House is meant.   He was a friend of Crabbe and Bowles, and for 33 years a member of Parliament.

[2] The Rev. George Bowles of Fawley. He was a cousin of Caroline.

[3] Evidently regarding his poem *Days Departed; or, Banwell Hill*. In the first edition (1828) Bowles relates (pp. 113–15) how as a boy going back to Winchester he had felt ashamed of his worsted boot-stockings, had spent a pound out of his one extra guinea for boots at Salisbury, and had then thrown the boot-stockings away. He retained the incident in the second edition (1829).

whose delineations of life and character are so beautiful and original, and whose poetry is so exquisitely affecting. Mrs. Bowles is equally charm'd with your stories, and most particularly with that of Blanche, which to read with dry eyes would be to read without a human heart.

Southey, I see, and I honor him for it, [h]as spoken of you in his last poem, or rather the dedication to it,[1] in a manner which does equal credit to both.

The description of fiends carrying off their victim —particularly when their forms become, slowly and darkly, visible—I think superior to any thing of the kind I have ever read. Give my kind regard to him, and say how happy I am that he holds his course so sublimely.

> While the dim raven clamors far below.

I grieve to think you have been so unwell, but trust the beautiful weather—which I welcome in my garden instead of in London, as I have done in London for forty-five years—will restore you sufficiently for you to drive over to Salisbury, should we be there, next February, and stay a few days with us.

Your letter came just time enough to save the romance of my new boots at Winchester, which I had put out, but it now abides, and when Banwell Hill next presents itself, you will consider I approach, and make my bow, in those new boots.

Notwithstanding, I fear the Bishop and Dean may think those boots con[trary] to the dignity of a shovel-hat !

Adieu, dear madam, and believe me
    Most faithfully your oblig'd friend,
            W. L. Bowles.

How does my old friend George ? You must know

---

[1] Southey published in 1829 the two long ballads *All for Love; and the Pilgrim of Compostella*. They contain a laudatory metrical dedication to Caroline Bowles.

E

that the great Paris publisher Galignani has written to say he intends publishing W. L. B.'s works![1]   This is what I never expected.   Moore has lost his interesting and beautiful daughter.[2]

Caroline Bowles to Bowles

BUCKLAND, *June 9th*, 1831.

My dear Sir,
        An unexpected pleasure awaited me at Fawley in the shape of your kind and valued present of " The Life of Bishop Ken,"[3] just put into my hands by George *our cousin*.

Accept my grateful thanks for the gift, and the pleasure I am *sure* of, from the perusal—for in the first place, being yours, it must be interesting and in the next I have seen samples of, and read comments on, the work which assure me I shall not be disappointed. Your *kind autograph* in the fly leaf is not in my estimation the least precious of the book's contents.

Some time since one of the County papers announced that " The Revd. W. L. Bowles " had withdrawn himself from the magisterial bench—and,

---

[1] A volume of selections from Milman, Bowles, Wilson, and Barry Cornwall was issued by Galignani in 1829.

[2] Anastasia Moore, born March 16, 1813, died March 8, 1829.

[3] Thomas Ken (1637–1711), Bishop of Bath and Wells, was one of the seven bishops imprisoned by James II.   In 1691, though he was not a violent non-juror, he was deprived of his See by William III. For a time he had lived with Isaac Walton, the husband of his half-sister.   His morning and evening hymns are well-known.

Bowles's *Life of Bishop Ken* appeared in two volumes in 1830–31. Caroline Bowles thought it might as well have been the life of the man in the moon, and Southey was deterred from reviewing it " by the certainty of mortifying him [Bowles], even if I totally abstain from noticing any of the faults in it, and only arrange his materials as he ought to have arranged them, and thrown his rubbish overboard." The omission precipitated Bowles's rebuke of Southey the following year.

would you believe it ?—I read the announcement with a feeling of satisfaction that was any thing but patriotic—for at whatever loss to the County, I could not but rejoice on your individual account that you had discharged yourself of a responsibility, " already become one of a most anxious nature," and in the progressive state of publick affairs too likely to be associated with the necessity of hazardous as well as harassing exertion.   Oh ! that there were some " happy Valley " to which we could flee away and be at peace !—some little spot of earth secure from political convulsion—wars and the rumours of wars, of pestilence, and famine, and all the horrors denounced against existing generations.

The portents are awful, but if England were true to herself I should still defy the world in arms against her.   Unhappily she turns a suicidal hand against herself and will He arrest it who alone has power ?

Kind *givers* sometimes make bold beggars.   " Please to remember the poor " when your 2nd volume of Ken comes out.

Ever, my dear sir,
Gratefully and affecly. yrs.,
CAR. A. BOWLES.

Bowles to Caroline Bowles

BREMHILL, *June 30th,* [1831].
My dear Madam,
The second volume of *our* Ken is before the public, and I hope will make its appearance with the author's best regards at Buckland, and moreover, I hope it will have better luck than its luckless author when he turn'd his unwilling poney from the door last summer.

. . . " So I beguile
The thing I am by seeming otherwise,"

in writing jocosely when every " third thought " is a
sigh, with you and Cowper,

> " Oh ! for a lodge in some vast wilderness."

But to quote my Shakespeare again,

> " Time and the hour run thro the roughest day."

I am coming to Salisbury on the 14th to preach to
eleven hundred children in the Cathedral, the children
of assembled village-schools, all orthodox, in these
days of heterodoxy !   " We," that is, I and the
Canoness, who is also turn'd author for the good of
the publick,[1] and our parish in particular, after resting
a day proceed to my *Lady Sister*, (Lady Williams) at
Portsmouth, and what if my *long tails* try their luck
at Buckland, instead of the poney-caravan ?

We think we could take you, in our road, going or
returning.   We have no house-hold at Salisbury in
the summer, or perhaps (who knows ?) might persuade
you to drive over and hold a plate at the Cathedral-
door, pour la charite, at eleven o'clock, on the fourteenth ?

In writing the life of a Bishop, contrary to the received custom, I have endeavour'd to vary a grave
subject by the interspersion, here and there, of matter
less grave ;   how the Dons (?) like it I do not know,
nor at all care :   my object was to give variety and
lightness to a rather heavy subject, for I am sure it
would not be read without, nor perhaps with it.

I have never had any connection with the Princes
of the Press, nor know a single writer among them
to wish me " good speed," and pen an article on
Bowles's Life of Ken ! and I fear Caroline Bowles,
with all her genius and powers of pathos, has no
Cavalier servante of the Press to usher her truthful
writings into the world's " garish eye," and yet, I

---

[1] *Characters and Incidents of Village Life* (1831).   Mrs. Bowles
published, in 1833 and 1836, two other moral pamphlets.

think, if our great and good friend, Southey, had said half as much as he feels, instead of parading, in the Quarterly, this stupid sentimental " Serving Man,"[1] he would have " done the state "—the state of literature, I mean—" more service."

However, we must throw " the bread on the waters," and let others pick up what chances to swim, when we are no more. Till that time, believe me,

Dear Madam,

Most truly, &c.,

W. L. BOWLES.

We thought it a duty to pay our respects to your friend, Lady Dalrymouth (?), the moment we return'd from Salisbury, tho we fear we have no right to hope she could be tempted from her seclusion.

Caroline Bowles to Bowles

BUCKLAND, 10*th July*, 1831.

My dear Sir,

Your *half* proposition about my coming to Salisbury to hear you preach for the charity on the 14th set me *wishing* I could do so. From wishing I got to planning, and then (the delicious summer weather making me bold and brave) I wrote to ask George if he would escort me. The reverend gentleman answers *yea*, comes over to me on Wednesday and, if the weather continues fine, we shall go on to Salisbury that evening and take up our quarters at the White Hart, to be in readiness for the Cathedral

---

[1] In 1831 Southey furnished an introduction to a volume of poems by an old butler, John Jones. He probably mentioned the volume in an article in the *Quarterly Review*. Moreover Mrs. Bray was about this time writing Southey accounts of the verse of a poor but well-born girl, Mary Colling ; Southey recommended publication and in March, 1832, reviewed the volume in the *Quarterly*. These circumstances incensed Bowles.

service on Thursday the 14th. Perhaps we may obtain a glimpse of you before that hour. At all events, afterwards I promise myself the pleasure of seeing you, and of an introduction to Mrs. Bowles, whom (I hope it is unnecessary for me to say) I shall be delighted to see at Buckland, if, by the help of your *long tails*, you favor me with the call you hint at in your way back from Portsmouth. I must add that if this delicious summer weather changes into wet and cold before the 14th I shall be most reluctantly obliged to give up my little excursion, being a very *summer* fly and shrinking like one from a cold blast. But I have *set my heart* on seeing you and your beautiful Cathedral, and you [know] when a woman's heart is set on any thing it goes hard with her but she brings it to pass. I am writing full gallop to save the post, so forgive this hurried scrawl.

My dear sir,

Yrs. most sincerely,

CAR. A. BOWLES.

Bowles to Caroline Bowles

CANONRY HOUSE, [SALISBURY],

July 13*th*, 1831.

My dear Madam,[1]

I received your kind note only yesterday— too late for me to write to you. We shall rejoice indeed if this finds you, and our only regret is that we have no household to offer such hospitalities as I could wish, the rooms being unfurnish'd, as I am not in residence, and the beds, except one, un-air'd.

[1] The letter is directed to Caroline at the White Hart, Salisbury. The next day in showing her the cathedral Bowles liberated two gentlemen who had been accidentally locked within it. Their mishap, and Caroline's remark that she would " have no objection to pass a moonlight night there quite alone," unnerved Bowles completely. Caroline wrote Southey on July 18, 1832, a very striking account of the incident.

Mrs. Bowles dines with Dr. Fowler. Mrs. Fowler is a name of ours—of my family, and yours, and you shall be taken such care of, as one of us, deserves so well. I can answer for this, so, if you ſtay to-morrow, as I hope you will, you will accompany Mrs. Bowles, and George can take my place, as it is probable I may be at the Bishop's.

I shall call this evening. If you come and I should not see [you], enquire to-morrow at church for Canon Bowles's ! closet, where you will find Mrs. Bowles and Fowler.

Ever &c.

Most truly,

W. L. BOWLES.

Bowles to Caroline Bowles

No. 178 PICCADILLY,

[*About June* 1, 1832.]

My dear Madam

I should have beg'd you acceptance of the enclos'd[1] much sooner, but waited till I came to town, for the sake of more dire&t and certain communication. These are not times to *publish such* poems, or any, but I have amus'd my own time, under much anxiety. I need not point out to whom I allude, in my preface, which, I hope, will be taken in good part, tho I could not avoid some notice of greater attention in distinguish'd literary journals, paid to disguſting and ſtupid bards of the *pantry* and *wash*-house, than to

---

[1] *St. John in Patmos*, published anonymously in 1832. In the preface Bowles laments that " the laureat Apollo of the living golden lyre " commends in a leading literary journal " a bashful livery-man " and " poetical sempstresses," while of " the elder living bards of Britain " and of such deserving young writers as J. F. Pennie (author of *Britain's Historical Drama*, 1832) " neglect, and almost utter critical silence, are the portion."

cultivated intellect and real genius. But the heart is sick with far more serious considerations.

God preserve us from the storm that seems impending, and believe me always

Most sincerely, &c.,

W. L. BOWLES.

Pray, make the corrections with the pen.

Caroline Bowles to Bowles

My dear Sir [1]   [*June 5*, 1832.]

Having lately seen in a provincial paper some extracts from a new poem entitled " St. John in Patmos," supposed to be written by you, I had just sent for the work, when your kind present put me in possession of the poem in a far more gratifying manner, as being the gift of its Author.

I have read it with deep interest and delight, acknowledging in heart and ear (?) the witchery of that harp of " one of the eldest living poets " which charmed my earliest youth, and having lost none of its powers to charm, affects me more profoundly now that I am myself entered on the evening path of life. We have both lived to see evil days, dark with signs and portents of worse to come—at least so seeming to our *shortsightedness*. But we know at least that the arm in which we trust is not shortened, and that oftentimes

> " The clouds we so much dread
> Are big with mercy, and may break
> In blessings on our head."

But for this confidence, I should be a coward indeed. You have chosen a glorious subject for your verse— beautifully appropriate to your profession and character, and many hearts there must be yet in England

[1] Directed to Bowles at No. 178, Piccadilly.

—even in this iron age—that will acknowledge with grateful admiration the undiminished powers of " the master of the spell."

I know that what you have written in allusion to *our* friend will in no ways affect the sincere regard he feels for you—tho' it may pain him to observe you are a little displeased with him. If I could by any magic sleight confine you here together for a day or two, I think that on more intimate acquaintance you would even forgive him for editing poor " John Jones." I must tell you and so would he, if you were to meet, that I am rather at variance with him as to the desirableness of drawing genius in low life (especially in women) before the publick except in some rare instances. I am a subscriber to *your* protégé —poor Pennie—and became so from really feeling that scant measure had been dealt to him of the praise to which he is so well entitled. But for *that poor man*, how much happier would he [line cut from letter] patronage drawn him from his obscurity,—to desert him when he had freighted his hopes on it ? I heard of you at Copthon's (?) and that you had missed George. You tantalize people cruelly. I would stay at home for six months in the hope of seeing you, but you " come like shadows, so depart." I am engaged, God willing, to be at Copthons (?) on the 14th of this month to stand sponsor to George's *little* Caroline Bowles. *You* will be remembered there and then— I answer for it—and will ever be most gratefully remembered by [last line and signature cut from letter].

Bowles to Caroline Bowles

PICCADILLY, *June 5th*, 1832.

My dear Madam
           I write under those impressions which I believe every serious person must feel as to our national

prospects at this momentous crisis, but I would not omit thanking you for your kind and interesting letter, and particularly because I would not, on any account, have your valued friend mis-understand me.

Most truly do I appreciate his benevolent and warm-hearted motives, but what astonishes me is that he should consider *such* poetry as he has brought forward, in the Quarterly Review, of Mary Dumpling a wit [whit ?] better than any other Mary could produce, which has not the advantage of being bad enough to laugh at ?   But, God forbid any thing I could say should, as you fear, for a moment " pain him," or that he should think, for one *half* of a moment, that I could dare to be " a little displeas'd with him."   Pray, only, if you think so, prevent his imagining this, and believe me

Ever most truly your oblig'd friend,
W. L. BOWLES.[1]

Remember me to the very Reverend George, of Fawley, and all there, and may little Caroline ever remember Caroline her sponsor.

[1] On June 9, 1832, Caroline Bowles informed Southey of Bowles's displeasure with him, speaking particularly of this letter as " so characteristic of his [Bowles's] infirmity of temper, and simplicity and real goodness of heart."   Southey replied July 4, 1832, that he had made complimentary references to Bowles in his articles, though Gifford had intercepted some of them.   " And now," he continued, " for your sake, if he does not come in my way, I will, on the first occasion, go out of mine to bring him in neck and shoulders."   Caroline, grateful for Southey's conciliatory attitude, discussed the question further on July 18th.   On the 30th Southey received from Bowles a copy of the poem, with an expression of personal goodwill.   He replied to Bowles cordially the same day, spoke of peculiar circumstances in regard to John Jones and Mary Colling which had caused him to notice them in his articles, and said he had endeavored, forty years before, to form his own style upon Bowles's.   (The letter is quoted in full in C. C. Southey : *Life and Correspondence of Robert Southey*, Vol. VI, pp. 192–94.)   On the 31st Southey reported all this to Caroline.   In her letter of thanks on August 20th she told him that Bowles was in high spirits and was talking of coming to see her.

Southey to Bowles

KESWICK, 4*th Oct.*, 1833.

My dear Sir

I am very much obliged to you and to Dr. Hawes; and had there been a house with the curacy, it would have appeared to me a most desirable situation for my son-in-law elect.[1]   Without one, it would be imprudent to accept it;—but we are not the less sensible of your kindness.

Next to a situation near my own abode, I should certainly prefer one in the west of England, as my *natale solum,*—whither my earliest, and therefore fondest recollections take their course when I give way to them;—and where some few of my old friends are still left.   Salisbury would have been for me a most desirable point to visit at, because of its position with regard to Bristol and Taunton,—and I may add to Buckland also,—a place which I shall never fail to visit while Caroline resides there, whenever I get as far south as London.   And for Mr. Warter it would have been not less so, because he would then have had opportunities of being known;—I do not say *making himself* known, because he is a person of no display; but of such sound learning, sound principles, and sound judgement, that were he placed where those qualifications could be seen, they could not fail to recommend him.

I have your Life of Ken, which I have read with the more interest because my mother's family claimed relationship with him.—I know not how, but I know that some seventy years ago there were thoughts of

---

[1] John Wood Warter (1806–78) had been chaplain to the English embassy at Copenhagen, 1830–33 ; but from just before his marriage (Jan. 15, 1834) to his death he was vicar of West Tarring, Sussex. He edited Southey's Commonplace Books, 4 volumes, 1849–1850, and *Selections from Southey's Letters,* 4 volumes, 1856.

sending her brother to Winchester, on that ground.—
You have made it a very amusing book; and it is no
slight recommendation of a biographical work when
it lets one as much into the character of the writer,
as of the subject. The whole of Ken's poems I have
read. His epics are certainly the most extravagant of
any that I have met with in any language; tho' there
are some Spanish and Portuguese ones which go far
in that way. But the most remarkable circumstance
relating to them is, that he kept pace with the march
of intellect in one direction, and made poetical use
(such as it was) of the scientific discoveries of his age.
For a poem half-serious, half-burlesque, like some of
the Italian, this sort of machinery would have been
excellently well adapted. Till I read Ken's Edmund
a Hymnothe I used to think Dr. Beaumont's Psyche
the oddest poem in the language.

. . . .

Moore's Irish Gentleman[1] has not been sent me.
Indeed I have been too closely employed upon Naval
History to have had time for any thing else. Next
week will give me a breathing time; and I shall make
use of it to prepare a paper for the Quarterly Review.
The Corn Law Poet[2] will furnish the text, and I shall
read him a wholesome but friendly lecture, upon the
mischievous direction which he has given to his extraordinary powers. He will know from whom it comes.
Many years ago he introduced himself to me by letter,
and sent me abundance of poems in which I saw so
much ability that I thought it worth while to bestow
upon him a good deal of instruction as to the art of
poetry, of which as an art he was utterly ignorant.
Such instruction could never have been better bestowed in one sense; but having acquired the art he

---

[1] Published in 1834. The *History of Ireland* occupied four
volumes and was not finished until 1846. It is unsatisfactory, and its
composition involved much unhappiness for Moore.
[2] Ebenezer Elliott (1781–1849).

has made perilous use of it.—When I have done with him, I may perhaps at the next interval of leisure think of Moore; but it is more likely that I shall wait for his History of Ireland in the Cabinet Cyclopædia. —Between Popery and Puritanism; a Whig ministry [tear in letter] and a Reformed Parliament; William 4th for our king and France for our ally, we are in a hopeful condition ! Yet—whatever national judgements may be necessary, not only as the strict consequence and just punishment of national sins, but as the means for bringing this nation to its senses, I have a steady trust in Providence that its judgements will be dispensed in mercy, and that the nation will be brought to its senses at last:—not however before you and I shall have become personally acquainted with Bishop Ken and his friend Piscator.

Have the goodness to express my sincerest thanks to Dr. Hawes, and believe me,

> My dear sir,
> Gratefully as well as truly yours,
> ROBERT SOUTHEY.

Southey to Bowles

KESWICK, *Sept.*, 1834.

My dear Sir [1]

In the course of this month I am about to leave home for a long circuit, with my son,[2]—an overgrown lad in his sixteenth year. My intention is to show him the house in which I was born, and the other scenes of my childhood, and then to visit some friends in the west, before I deposit him with his brother-in-law,

---

[1] This is the lost letter from Southey regarding Coleridge. It reveals an alienation sufficiently great, but not so bitter as the imperfect recollection of it in Moore's *Diary* (February 20, 1835) implies.

[2] Charles Cuthbert Southey (1819–88). He published Southey's *Life and Correspondence*, 6 volumes, 1850.

in Sussex, to be prepared for Oxford. Should you
be at Bremhill about the second week in October,
and you can conveniently receive us, I would gladly
take the opportunity,—which may never again occur,
—of passing two days with you.

I saw your letter in the Times concerning poor
Coleridge,[1] and can tell you more circumstances concerning his campaign. What papers he has left I have
not yet been informed: there will probably be little
or nothing in a finished state,—but many notes and
fragments. His nephew Henry Nelson Coleridge has
for several years been in the habit of noting down
what he could bear away of his conversation; and it
is very likely that some of his disciples may have done
the same. With these materials, and his correspondence, there may be a considerable quantity of unpublished remains.

His relations were proud of his reputation, but had
no other feeling connected with him. Living wholly
for himself as he had so long done, his death has
brought with it little grief and no loss to any of them.
There was a time when I should have thought it the
greatest that could have befallen me. It has now
forcibly recalled old recollections. Forty years have
elapsed since our first meeting,—and one consequence
of that meeting has been that I have resided during
the last thirty in this place, whither I first came with no
other intention than that of visiting him. In this and
in all other things a gracious Providence has disposed
of me much better than, if my own hopes and prospects had been fulfilled, I should have disposed of
myself.

The General [Peachey ?] is expected here in the
course of the autumn, but is not likely to make any
long tarriance, for his own house will not be in a
state to receive him. It has undergone a radical
reform, whereby much deformity has been produced

<hr>

[1] Published August 13, 1834.

at great expence; and (except in an increase of room) with the least possible convenience.   Mrs. P. has also undergone a reform; she has become *evangelical*, —and the poor General when he arrives will be taken to sit under many a dolorous lecture,—where if his slumbers do him no good, nothing else will.—This parish is unhappily being divided into sheep and goats, by a well-educated and well meaning, but in this respect most injudicious curate: and Mrs. P. who probably looks forward to making this her place of abode, will be the leader of the sheep.

Farewell, my dear sir, and believe me always

Yours with sincere regard,

ROBERT SOUTHEY.

Southey to Bowles

KESWICK, 25 *Sept.*, 1834.

My dear Sir

I received both your kind notes,—and have now to make a sad reply to them.   My plans are all disconcerted.   Long insomnolence has brought my wife to such a state that it is impossible for me to leave her.[1]   If it please God, I will visit you in the spring;[2]—meantime I must remain here, and abide the event, trusting to his mercy, and looking to Him for support.

[Signature cut from letter.]

---

[1] She lived until November, 1837.

[2] His only visit to Bremhill was made from a Saturday until the following Wednesday between November 10 and November 16, 1836.

Southey to Bowles

BUCKLAND, 11 *Jany.*, 1837.

My dear Sir [1]

Here I have found your most friendly invitation to Salisbury, and here your letter of the 9th to Caroline has found me. Few things would have pleased me more than to pass a few days as agreeably with you in your residence in the Close, as I did at Bremhill. But this cannot be. The time of my absence from home has already been inconveniently extended, tho many things which I wish to do have been left undone, and tho the pleasure of meeting an old friend has been too quickly followed by the pain of saying farewell to him.

Since we left you we have travelled more than a thousand miles, zigzagging by highroads and byroads, from the north coaſt to the south, and from the south coaſt to the north, and here we now are upon the south again. What the weather has been you know. The tornado caught us at Dawlish, the snow ſtorm at Tavistock; and a ſtorm of thunder, rain and wind, which might have demolished us had it come on a quarter of an hour sooner, when we were on the cliff-path, did us no other harm than drenching us in the Valley of Stones. In all this journey we have neither met with impediment, delay, or mishap of any kind. We have been at Hartland point, at Clovelly, at Bude, Boscaſtle and Tintagel, and in a cavern there whence there came forth an icey wind like to Sarsar: we have been at the Land's End, have visited St. Michael's chair, and the Well of St. Keyne's, and have seen the again half-buried British church at Peranzabuloe, a scene which fills one with sad emotions as Stonehenge alone, of all the remarkable objeéts with which I am

[1] Directed to Salisbury.

acquainted, can excite. The difference is that you have here a Christian place of worship, and a desert of sand. If sight-seeing had been our only object, this place alone (where there is so little to see, and so much that may be imagined) would have repaid us.

I have seen Mary Colling also, and to see her would have been worth a longer journey, for I never saw any one more happily circumstanced in that state and station of life in which his or her place has been assigned,—nor more remarkable for perfect propriety in her whole demeanour. She told me of a Miss Beckford to whom she performed the last office of humanity at Tavistock, and who used to talk much to her of you, as you ought to be talked of, and promised to give her your poems. After her death Mary looked after her effects till some connection arrived, and by so doing she procured for them a considerable sum. . . .

But the main object of my journey was to see once more the few friends whom I have left, in the western part of England:—a sort of duty (and of no mean degree) which one owes to one's self and to them.

My strength and spirits (thank God) have proved equal to a circuit which has tried them both. But I long to be at rest, and to resume my habitual occupation and way of life. This cannot be before the middle of February;—for I have at least a fortnight's business in London, a week to pass with my daughter in Sussex, —and other movements, which with odds and ends of affairs will consume ten days more. There is a world of work before me on my return but happily I am never so cheerful as when I am most actively employed, and can say at night, " Sufficient for the day hath been the business thereof."

God bless you, my dear sir. My son joins with me in thankful remembrances to Mrs. Bowles. When I come again into these parts, I will not fail to visit you

F

again, God willing, whether you are at Bremhill, or Salisbury.

　　　　Believe me always,
　　　　　　Yours with affectionate regard,
　　　　　　　　ROBERT SOUTHEY.

Caroline looks less ill than when I saw her in Feb., 1835. Her faithful servant is glad to hear me say so, especially because others who see her also but seldom, and at considerable intervals of time, have made a like remark. Her excellent spirits and excellent principles support her, in a situation where she feels the loss of all those persons in whose society she had most enjoyment. She desires me to send her kind remembrances.

Southey to Bowles

My dear Mr. Bowles [1]　KESWICK, 25 *Apr.*, 1837.

　　I am much obliged to you for your letter, and for your friend Mr. Harford's beautiful book, which came to me some days ago in a frank from the Home Office. It is well that any thing good can come from that office in these times.

　　I have also to thank you for the honour which you intend me in your forthcoming edition,—a very great honour I cannot but consider it, especially remembering (what I shall never forget) the improvement as well as the delight which I derived from your poems more than forty years ago, and have acknowledged in a general preface (just drawn out) to my own.[2] The

---

　[1] This letter, which is directed to Salisbury, is printed in Vol. VI (pp. 332–34) of the *Life and Correspondence of Robert Southey.* That version, however, varies somewhat in punctuation from this; omits the first paragraph; and softens the opening of the fifth paragraph to " The men who are now in power," etc.

　[2] The collected edition of Southey's poetry appeared in 1837–38. The preface contains an acknowledgment of the delight and benefit Southey had received from Bowles.

Conscript Fathers of the Row have set me upon a collected edition of them.

The booksellers in one respect have rendered me a service by accelerating what I had looked forward to as a posthumous publication: for I might otherwise have deferred the necessary preparations, waiting for a more convenient season, till it would have been too late. Indeed it requires some resolution to set about a task which brings in review before me the greater part of my life,—old scenes, old feelings, and departed friends. No doubt the reason why so many persons who have begun to write their own lives, have stopt short when they got thro' the chapter of their youth, is that the recollections of childhood and adolescence tho' they call up tender thoughts, excite none of that deeper feeling with which we look back upon the time of life when wounds heal slowly, and losses are irreparable.

The mood in which I have set about this revision is like that a man feels when he is setting his house in order. I waste no time in attempting to mend pieces that are not worth mending: but upon Joan of Arc which leads the way, as having first brought me into notice, a good deal of patient labour has been bestowed. The faults of language have been weeded out, and as many others as it was possible to extirpate. This would have been a preposterous attempt if the poem had been of a piece before; but it was written in 1793, rewritten in 1795, and materially altered in 1797, and what has been done now makes the diction of the same character throughout. Faults enough of every other kind remain to mark it for a juvenile production.

The miscreants who are now in power are doing the greatest injury they can to the Church, by strengthening the only strong argument that can be brought against the alliance between Church and State. *They* certainly overlook all considerations of character, station, acquirements, and desert in the disposal of their preferment, and regard nothing but the interest of their own party, the very vilest that has ever disgraced this country. It will tend to confirm the American Episcopalians in the only point upon which they differ from their English brethren, and I am more sorry for this than for the handle which it gives to the Dissenters at home;—for in these dark times the brightest prospect is that of the Episcopal Church in America,—and yet without an alliance with the State, and endowments for learned and laborious leisure, it never can be all that a Church ought to be.

I am a good hoper, even when I look danger full in the face. We are now in great danger of a severer dearth than any within our memory. Here in Cumberland at this time there is scarcely the slightest appearance of spring, last year the hay failed, and the sheep are now dying for want of food. . . . Mischief of course is at work in the manufacturing countries, and it will be tremendously aided by the New Poor Laws, which are not more useful in some of their enactments than they are inhuman in others.—I fear however nothing so much as a premature change of Ministry; let the present men remain to reap what they have sown.—You and I cannot live to see the issue of all these changes that are in prospect,—but as an old man in this neighborhood said, " Mayhap we may hear tell ! "

God bless you, my dear sir. Present my kind regards to Mrs. Bowles, and believe me,

Yours affectionately,
Robert Southey.

Southey to Bowles

London, 25*th Aug.*, 1838.

My dear Sir

Circumstances have so far influenced my projected movements that instead of passing, as I had intended, a few days at Bremhill on my outward bound course, I must make that port on my return in the autumn. We are six fellow-travellers, and the convenience of five must be consulted, accounting my son in such matters as one with myself. Here I am in this modern Babylon, to me always the most odious of all places. On Monday next we depart for Dover.

Your sonnet[1] gave me very great pleasure, both for its intrinsic worth and for the gratifying reflection that my chance meeting with a lady whom heaven knows I never desired to meet, should have been the means of bringing the sweet sounds of the country again within your reach.—I wish I were out of reach of the abominable noise of the town, never again to hear it.

I have to thank you for your Discourses on the Cartoons[2] which I found yesterday lying for me at my brother's in Harley Street.

I passed a few days with Caroline, " my dear friend and sister poetess." You will be glad to hear that she is in better health than usual, better indeed than she has known for several years. We had some delightful walks together, for she is able to walk six or seven miles without fatigue. One very remarkable place she took me to, a few miles from Lymington; it is called Shirley holmes, and appears at a distance like a circular grove; upon entering it, you come into a large circular glade with four roads leading into it. I had never heard of it before, nor do I know whether it is mentioned in any account of the New Forest; but the first supposition which occurs is that it may

[1] Bowles contributed to the *Gentleman's Magazine* for July, 1838, a sonnet entitled " On a Trumpet for Deafness." It was accompanied by the statement : " Recommended by Mr. Southey, who said ' You will again hear the birds sing, the bees hum, and the waters flow.' "

[2] William IV presented Lansdowne with copies of the cartoons of Raphael for use in Bowood Chapel. Bowles preached upon these a series of sermons, which he issued collectively in 1838.

have [been] a Druidical grove: that it must have been formed for some special purpose cannot be doubted.

I am now in the bustle of preparing and packing for our journey. Normandy and Bretagne are the provinces which we propose to visit, turning aside perhaps to see La Vendée. There is a great pleasure in travelling over historical ground, however uninteresting the face of the country may be. But these parts of France I believe are beautiful in themselves as well as interesting from the events which have taken place there in elder and in later times. Hitherto it has been my practice whenever I went abroad, or made any long journey in the remoter parts of my own country, to keep a full journal. Few things require so much resolution as to set about this every day in spite of fatigue and the temptations of society. Yet at my time of life whatever is not noted down while the impression is fresh must be soon forgotten. So I shall endeavour to keep up the practice of my youth.

Present my kindest remembrances to Mrs. Bowles, and believe me, my dear sir,

Yours with affectionate regard,

ROBERT SOUTHEY.

Southey to Bowles

BUCKLAND, 27 *Nov.*, 1838.

My dear Sir

I had been devising how and when and where to find my way to you, and whether at Bremhill or at Salisbury. Time was when I thought myself an experienced traveller, and had no difficulty in striking across the country from one part of England to another. But railways have altered all this, and the best book of the roads is now as obsolete as a last year's almanack. Meantime days and weeks have past by, and in their course, my purpose of seeing you in Wiltshire has been laid aside.   You will hold me excused for this when I tell you that your cousin Caroline has consented to contract a nearer relationship with me.[1] After one and twenty years of more than ordinary intimacy, during which no thought of any such possibility could ever have been entertained, we have agreed to pass the remainder of our days together, believing that no persons could be better suited to each other in all essential points.

You will not wonder then that I have not advanced beyond Buckland since my return from France.   And it is more becoming that you should be made acquainted with our engagement directly from me, than that you should hear of it some time hence through a newspaper.

Caroline desires me to add her very kind regards.

Believe me, my dear sir,

Yrs. with sincere regard and esteem,

ROBERT SOUTHEY.

[1] They were married June 4, 1839.

Crabbe to Bowles

TROWBRIDGE, *Feb.* 19, 1815.

Dear Sir [1]

After I had the pleasure of seeing you and Mrs. Bowles, I went with some degree of apprehension to his Lordship the Bishop, and as I supposed my punishment would be reproof in some form of words (though to you and you only I held myself accountable) I was not prepared for that which awaited me: " His Lordship is not well enough to see you, sir." Now this is as it should be: had the Bishop of Meath received me graciously, I had felt some kind of self-reproach, such as I feel when I think of my offence to you, but after this his Lordship and I ſtand on equal terms and I have no apology to make and perhaps if I had, no opportunity of making it would occur.

But this is an incidental business. My principal reason for thus troubling you is to beg your excuse for leaving you on Tuesday evening. A friend from Trowbridge accompanies me to Bath or joins me there, and as I shall be three or four days at our inn it will be more convenient for me at once to take our rooms, and indeed I have promised to meet him on our return from our several engagements, nor will this deprive me of the pleasure of your society for any portion of that evening nor occasion any other difference than two minutes' walk from your house to the inn.

[1] Directed to Bath. Crabbe had some difficulty with his predecessor at Trowbridge regarding the tithes; but in this letter he seemingly refers rather to a social breach of some minor sort at Bath.

It gave me much satisfaction to learn that our distance is not so great as to forbid my reasonable hope of seeing you and Mrs. Bowles at this parsonage. Much I cannot promise, but I can truly say that I shall be very glad to see you and will endeavour to procure for you the company of Mr. Smith and any friend you may have in our vicinity. Have the goodness to say everything grateful to Mrs. Bowles and accept my best thanks yourself for the good-humoured forgiveness I received from both. It has almost reconciled me to my offence, which however I must thus far extenuate as to assure you that I was taken by surprise and had not due time for recollection. And yet you must not [tear in MS.] this to my very obliging friends who make their houses so agreeable to me.

Yours, dear sir,

Very truly,

GEO. CRABBE.

Crabbe to Bowles

TROWBRIDGE, 24 July, 1815.

My dear Sir

Your kindness distresses me; innocent as in fact I am, I nevertheless feel as if I had occasioned you (and that wilfully) trouble and disappointment. I was greatly mortified at Bath, where I soon heard that you sought me, though not till some days after, in whose company it was that you did me this honour.

Heaven knows, my dear sir, the pleasure that I should promise to myself in such company as you mention and at such place, but I doubt the possibility of being so gratified. My sons are not with me and I have no unengaged neighbours among the clergy, though the curate of Hilperton might perhaps baptise an infant or marry a couple for me; but if I visited Bremhill by that mode of conveyance you have ordered, does it follow that I can return in the same way ? Nor is it requisite, if I can order a chaise from Chippenham, and why not do this to Bremhill, instead of giving trouble to you ? But all this may be determined when I am favoured by the promised call in the latter end of the present week. Be assured, dear sir, of this, that I shall not *easily* relinquish the pleasure of joining your party and I wish very much to thank the Marquis of Lansdowne for the honour he does me. The Marchioness I may hope to see at some future time. I have been as solitary as a busy man can be conceived to be. . . . Doleful matters render me at once desirous of such comfort as you hold forth and unfit me for it. . . .

I will inform Col. Houlton of what you mention. Will you present my respectful and kind wishes to Mrs. Bowles, and will you accept my best thanks yourself ?

I am, my dear sir,
Yours truly, &c.,
GEO. CRABBE.

Crabbe to Bowles

TROWBRIDGE, 20 Oct., 1817.

My dear Sir

I am in the midst of business which has been accumulating for a month past and during that time I have been gossiping with idle people of both sexes at Sidmouth. I mean nevertheless to escape from the claims of these small affairs and though I cannot dine with you on Wednesday I fully purpose to meet you at Chippenham on the next day.

Thanks for your invitation. I was mortified to receive three such notes from Mr. Methuen and to know that Mr. Rogers was in this part of the country and I shut up with every-day people in Devonshire (with one exception, however). But there is no good in this retrospection. I will think of the pleasure of meeting you at Chippenham.

Yours faithfully,

GEO. CRABBE.

Crabbe to Bowles

TROWBRIDGE, 23 *Nov.*, 1827.

My dear Sir

Your letter was obliging and friendly and truly yours. I thanked you heartily, but I did not think it necessary to trouble you with acknowledgments of which you would not doubt, but kindly give me credit for them. My son too returns his thanks. These, however, you would have been spared, had it not occurred to me some few hours since that my silence is not becoming, but that I ought to express my sense of that other part of your letter in which you do me the honour of communicating your sentiments and purposes respecting the imprisonment of Mrs. Cook, and I judge it right to declare my opinion on the subject, which is that you have done nobly and courageously, as a gentleman, a man, and a Christian, and I might add as a magistrate and a priest, taking it for a fact that the sentence last inflicted upon the poor woman could not be mitigated by the same authority and power by which it was pronounced.

The public opinion is, I think, expressed in the Morning Herald. Other papers I do not see, except the provincial, but men (and surely women) must sympathise in the sufferings of a person so aged and with such general character as this their fellow-sinner. Having satisfied my own feelings by thus declaring them,

I remain, my dear sir,

Very cordially yours,

GEO. CRABBE.

Crabbe to Bowles

TROWBRIDGE, 28 *April*, 1828.

My dear Sir

You have taught me to ask favours by kindly complying when I sought them and you find how soon I repeat my requests. You are going to town and perhaps within a few days and if so will you indulge me by receiving for me the medal voted to me by the council of the R. S. of Literature ? It is in the possession of the Honbl. Mr. G. A. Ellis, M.P., Spring Garden, and I have ventured to inform him that you will do me the honour of conveying it to me. For this purpose and at your own time I will trouble you to do this business for me, and as paper is not sufficiently defensive against accidents, I will thank you to give me credit for so much money as will purchase a small box of any material hard enough to bear pressure, and lastly (as your return will not be within two or three weeks ?) I must beg of you to order the parcel to be directed to

Your much obliged Sevt.,

GEO. CRABBE.

Crabbe to Bowles

TROWBRIDGE, 2*nd May*, 1828.

My dear Sir

I heartily thank you for your kindness to oblige me by taking trouble upon yourself and I should be glad to be informed by what means I might be of use to you, though in honest truth I begin to feel that I cannot be very useful to any one.

The reason for my not mentioning the History of Bremhill[1] was this. I had not read at that time more

---

[1] *The Parochial History of Bremhill* was the outgrowth of Bowles's agreement to furnish a topographical sketch of the parish for Sir Richard C. Hoare's *Modern Wiltshire*. It treated a variety of topics.

than a very few pages: I knew nothing of Wansdike,
nothing of Tanhill, and could not have told in what
county, scarcely in what kingdom, were Avebury and
Silbury. I was called from my own room (where I
read now, and once studied) when I left Bremhill till
my return. On my return a letter from an old friend
and contemporary, the Rector of Yarmouth in Norfolk,
again summoned me from this depository of my books
and fossils, both lying in curious disorder, and only
three days have past since I could fairly say I had
arrived at the knowledge of " parochial psalmody
and church-yard inscriptions," concluding with that
exquisite morsel of improvement on the epitaph of the
old couple. Indeed that is the true and long approved
stone-cutter style and I wonder that you would produce
anything so utterly unlike it.

I am not a reader of topography, though at one time
I corresponded with John Nichols.[1] I always had an
opinion that it was extremely dull and I even now
suspect that yours is not the genuine sort, for I understand you very well and to say nothing of knowledge
acquired, have been amused. The account of parishes
and their " fat rectors " is most assuredly correct,
lamentably correct. Still it is better that we should
be abused for the vices which they impute to us than
for any real likeness to their odious pictures.

Your natural history and more especially your
account of Kelloway rock[2] revived in me the desire
of seeing that part of the county, but there must be
another revival before I can indulge myself. I want
strength and steadiness. Looking upward is the sure
cause of a distressing giddiness, which I am willing
to impute to ill digestion, and my medical friend is
willing that I should.

I read the more learned portion of the work with

[1] Editor of the *Gentleman's Magazine.* He collaborated with
Bowles in *The Annals and Antiquities of Lacock Abbey.*
[2] A shelly limestone, described by Bowles on p. 162.

all the interest I could acquire and really by the time I had finished the notes on Chap. 2nd I conceived that I understood the matter, like a contributor to the Gentleman's Magazine.   I mean in its pristine glory: I do not see it at this time. . . . You feel and in places raise feelings in your reader.   But this accords not with topography.   He who writes concerning monuments of all or any kind, if I may judge by the little I read of them, should have no more of feeling than the things themselves.   Cold, stern judges of dead and decayed materials for investigation.   Perhaps I err and Sir R. C. Hoare might correct my opinion. But seriously, though I like your book the better because it engages me by subjects which I partly understand, yet I dare not affirm that a rigid antiquary would approve any portion of the work, except that which I either do not comprehend or cannot relish. . . .

I have written more than I purposed but not all I had to observe, which however you will have no cause to lament.

I repeat my thanks for your kind assent to my request and am, with cordial good wishes and respect to Mrs. Bowles, Your obliged and obedt. Sert.,

GEO. CRABBE.

My friend from Norfolk spoke of a late affair[1] from the papers which he saw and with mind wholly un-prejudiced is decidedly with us.   He is also a magis-trate but thinks not with our brethren at Devizes.

George Crabbe the Younger to Bowles

PUCKLECHURCH, *August* 5, 1833.

Revd. and dear Sir

Do not think me ungrateful.   I have been endeavouring to procure a true copy of the inscription

---

[1] The censure of Bowles regarding Catherine Cook.

for my father's monument, as you wished to see it, but I am sorry to say I cannot engage for the accuracy of the following transcript, as I believe some alteration was made afterwards contrary to the desire of Mr. Rogers, who does not wish that it should be considered as his own.

" Sacred to the memory of the Revd. George Crabbe, L.L.B. who died Feby. 3rd, 1832, in the eighteenth year of his services as rector of this parish and in the 78th year of his age.

. . . . . .

Born in humble life, he made himself what he was: With the force of his genius he broke thro' the obscurity of his birth; yet never ceased to feel for the less fortunate, entering into the sorrows and deprivations (as his Works will testify) of the poorest of his parishioners.

As a writer, he is well described by a contemporary and eminent poet—

' Tho Nature's sternest painter, yet her best.'[1]

. . . . . .

This monument is erected to his memory by some of his affectionate friends and parishioners."

I am doubtful whether there be not some error, because I have only an imperfect copy of the inscription, but as it will be placed in Trowbridge chancel about the 8th of this month, the papers will probably mention the circumstance and give an accurate transcript of the epitaph. It was debated by the subscribers at Trowbridge whether it should be written in Latin or English. If the former had been adopted you were to have been requested to compose it; but it was decided (and I think judiciously) that it should be in English, and was drawn up accordingly by the principal subscribers and sent to Mr. Rogers for his correction,

[1] From *English Bards and Scotch Reviewers*.

and he and Lord Holland had the goodness to send
the above, which has been somewhat altered, but I
cannot precisely say where the variation lies.   It is
certainly very different in expression if not in meaning
from the one which was written at Trowbridge—
more concise and polished.

.   .   .   .

I returned [from my visit to you] improved in health
and exulting in spirit on account of the kindness and
honour I received.   When [shall] I exult still more in
seeing you all seated at my homely table ?   I will copy
Westerlush (?) as soon as I have the inexpressible
pleasure of writing the last word in my Memoir. . . .
Pray present my very grateful remembrances to Mrs.
Bowles and believe me, dear sir,

Yours faithfully and respectfully,

G. CRABBE.[1]

Pray tell your dear and excellent lady that I have
not forgotten the flowers nor will forget them, tho I
earnestly hope she will come and choose for herself.
I want to write about the books I carried home with
me, but I have no room.

George Crabbe the Younger to Bowles

PUCKLECHURCH, *Nov.* 11*th*, 1833.

Revd. and dear Sir
I return the letter you allowed me to copy
with many thanks.   I fear you will repent having begun
to confer favours upon me when you find I grow more
importunate the more I receive.   A gentleman connected with the Albemarle establishment has been
here, who brings very pleasing intelligence respecting
the progress and prospects of the New Edition of my

---

[1] This son of the poet was curate of Pucklechurch, Gloucestershire,
and afterwards rector of Bradfield, Suffolk.

father's Works, including my narrative now under the correcting hands of Mr. Lockhart.[1] He tells me that Mr. Rogers and Mr. Lockhart lately passed a morning together conversing about the publication and that they and Mr. Moore have actually designed to crown the Memoir by noting down any remark or incident they remember relative to my father in the form of a letter directed to me. I have been encouraged therefore by their kindness and condescension to address the same request to Professor Wilson, Mr. Southey, and several more of my father's most eminent friends which I now prefer to you.[2] Do, dear sir, join your celebrated friends in this good work. Take up your pen on the spur of the occasion, for I know the facility with which it can run over some anecdote such as the delightful one you told me respecting the poets at Bowood, or any incident or remark that occurs to your mind—your first or after impressions of my father or such-like—when you have met him in public or private. I know how easily you can do this without the least labour or thought, or I would not ask it lest I should infringe upon the time that ought to be wholly devoted to Bremhill 2nd &c., which it would be sacrilege to invade.

With such additions and Mr. Lockhart's correction, the Narrative will, I *now* believe, be placed beyond any fear of a failure, with which I should be very sorry to connect your name. The Prospectus will show you we are very rapidly approaching the hour of publication.

I am, dear sir,
Your faithful and obliged Sert.,
GEORGE CRABBE.

I have received the first chapter from the press.

[1] Lockhart took a good many liberties with the *Life*, even altering some of the letters that were quoted.

[2] Bowles is not among those whom young Crabbe, in his preface, mentions by name as drawing up summaries of personal reminiscences.

G

Bowles to Murray

SALISBURY, [*Feb.*, 1834].

My dear Sir

I had already order'd three copies of poor Crabbe's moſt intereſting, moſt affecting, and beautifully written Life, and am induc'd by the kind present and kinder notice from the publisher, sent to Calne, to inform you of two rather singular circumſtances; but I muſt firſt say that the laſt copy, being sent to Calne, inſtead of Salisbury, where I am present resident, was not received till a few days ago, and Mrs. Bowles, who is now again reading it, only this morning discover'd the kind note from the publisher.

I haſten therefore to thank you, dear sir, for this remembrance, and now muſt tell you what passed with regard to the firſt copy I purchased.

I had read the volume all thro, and being deeply intereſted, I wrote a letter to Crabbe of Pucklechurch, because I thought it would give him pleasure, being a young author. I recommended the volume warmly to the Bishop, Dean, and all here, and sent the letter to G. Crabbe for the Bishop to frank. It was not till afterwards I accidentally look'd at the front leaf, which I had not perceiv'd, and found my name and the very beautiful dedication.[1]

As I had written without saying one word about the dedication, I inſtantly poſted off another letter, as the author would naturally suppose I was displeas'd or ungrateful, when I could hardly read it without tears; and now, tho late, beg to thank you for your kind remembrance, as I cordially thank'd him. I have only to add my earneſt hope that the work, if

[1] " To the Rev. W. L. Bowles, Canon of Salisbury, &c., &c., &c., these Memoirs of his Departed Friend and Brother-Poet Are Inscribed, in Testimony of that Grateful and Affectionate Respect, Which Has Descended from Mr. Crabbe to his Children's Children."

there is any true feeling in poetry in England, will repay you for your liberality and the interest you have taken.[1]

Crabbe most gratefully spoke of the few services I was able to do to his lamented Father, of which I was scarce conscious, and propos'd dedicating the first volume to me, but I earnestly pressed him, tho deeply feeling the kindness of the intention, to dedicate it to Lord Holland, or some name which might be of eventual (?) advantage to him, and therefore thought no more of it, but his high disinterestedness prevail'd, notwithstanding which I do hope the suggestion in the Quarterly will be soon realis'd.[2]

I beg to be remember'd to Mr. Lockhart, whom I met last at poor Sotheby's table, since which I have not been in London. These things come near us at all times but more at a certain age. I shall hope to see him and yourself in the spring, and would beg the favour of you, if you will allow it, to advertise in your Quarterly list my corrected edition of St. John in Patmos, with my name, and believe me,

Most sincerely,

W. L. Bowles.

Advertise also to be published Antiquities of Lacock Nunnery.

You never had an article on Cathedral Music. Ask Mr. Lockhart if I shall send one, for him to do as he likes with.[3] I think it a most interesting subject in these times, and I am able historically and practically to speak of it, and should like the task.

Every body here speaks in the highest terms of the Life, particularly the Dean.

[1] Murray was publisher of young Crabbe's edition (8 volumes, 1834) of the *Poetical Works* of his father.

[2] In its treatment of Vol. I of the *Poetical Works*, the *Quarterly Review* expressed the hope (January, 1834) that young Crabbe would not long remain a curate.

[3] The article, if sent, was not published.

Moore to Bowles

My dear Bowles   *Wednesday,* [*April,* 1819].

Many thanks for the offer of the Blackwood, but I am quite satisfied with knowing that they don't abuse me, and, still more, with your kindness in hastening to tell me so. You don't forget, I hope, that we are to go together to the Anacreontic[1] (that vile epithet, as you call it, for us elderly gentlemen). I shall be at [illegible] at whatever hour you appoint in the morning of that day, and Bessy considers herself as invited to go too. I have written to Sir John Stevenson,[2] who is in London, to ask him to come down.

Yours ever,
T. Moore.

Your pamphlet is unanswerable,[3] but I fear the public will not read. Corn Laws and the Currency will beat you out of the field.

Moore to Bowles

My dear Bowles,—   *Thursday Eve.*

I have written to Doctor Bain to say that you are coming. He gave me full powers last time (you

---

[1] A society at Bath. Perhaps named for Moore's translation of Anacreon.

[2] Sir John Andrew Stevenson (1760?–1833). He wrote the accompaniments to Moore's *Irish Melodies.*

[3] *The Invariable Principles of Poetry*, an answer to Campbell's attack upon Bowles's edition of Pope. Bowles had left a copy of the pamphlet at Sloperton on April 23, 1819.

know) to take advantage of any " mollia tempora " I might see in you towards visiting him. He will therefore expect you, and you must not leave me in the lurch. As to his having *room*, he expects Mrs. Moore and all the little ones, and therefore you can easily be stowed away in their place. Besides I have bid him put me in his *worst* Poet's Corner.

We must set off Tuesday or Wednesday at the very farthest. Let me have a line.

Yours, &c.,
T. MOORE.

Moore to Bowles

Wednesday, [May, 1824].

My dear Bowles—¹

My only reason for taking my book to you was that I thought (of the two) you had better read *me, myself*, than the misrepresentations of me in John Bull and Blackwood—and if I had stayed a little longer with you, I think I should have forced you to swallow at least a chapter or two, as physic. Not that I believe you to *want* physic of any sort or kind, as you will confess yourself before you are a week in London.

I mean to start on Saturday and shall be on the watch for you next week.

Yours ever most truly,
THOMAS MOORE.

¹ On May 1, 1824, Moore went to Bremhill and laughed Bowles out of a state of nervousness and apprehension from which he had suffered for at least a week. Bowles refused, however, to read a copy of *Captain Rock* which Moore had brought for his perusal. " He will read the abuse [of it in reviews] readily enough," wrote Moore in his *Diary*, " though he won't read the book."

Moore to Bowles

My dear Bowles,   *Saturday Night.*

I should have answered your note sooner,
but that I expected to meet you at [illegible]'s dance
the other night, where I am sorry you and Mrs.
Bowles did not attend. How are we to come together?
I have been in town since I saw you, and want to tell
you about the pangs of Rogers's parturition, which I
witnessed. As to the Quarterly Review, it does you
honour—as it shows you are not *partizan* enough to
suit the tastes of those *ultra* gentlemen.[1]

Yours very truly,

THOMAS MOORE.

Moore to Bowles

My dear Sir—   *Saturday Night.*

I said that, if you did not hear from me to the
contrary, you might depend upon us for Monday next,
but I think it is as well to let you know that we are
perfectly at your disposasl for that day, if you are able
to send the carriage for us. I find Crabbe is to be at
Bowood this next week, and I wish our meeting there
(as, of course, we shall all be asked " poetis nos laeta-
mur *tribus* ") could be arranged for one of the days
we meant to pass with you.—Jeffrey has been very
kind to me in the Review just come out—indeed most
generously so, considering all he had said before.[2]

Yours, my dear Bowles (may I say so ?) very truly,

THOMAS MOORE.

---

[1] The *Quarterly Review* attacked Bowles in July, 1820, with regard
to his criticisms of Pope. In October, 1825, it attacked him a second
time. The reference is conjecturally to one or the other of these
articles, more likely the former.

[2] In July, 1806, Moore and Jeffrey met, somewhat farcically, upon
the field of honor : officers interfered, and it was discovered that
Jeffrey's pistol was not loaded. The two men afterwards became good
friends. Moore is of course here referring to some notice in the
Edinburgh Review.

Moore to Bowles

SLOPERTON,
Friday.

My dear Bowles—

In consequence of my having consented to become arbiter between Sir J. Stevenson and his publisher, (in order to prevent *them* too from going to logger-heads) I laſt night received an immense packet of the Knight's Music to sit in judgment upon, which will make it impossible, I fear, for me to go to Brem-hill before the Sothebys leave you. I regret this moſt heartily, but so it is, and I cannot help it. Give my beſt regards to Mr. Sotheby.

If it should be fine on Monday, and my task is entirely got through, I may perhaps walk over to you and ſtay the night.

Ever yours,
T. MOORE.

Moore to Bowles

March 24, 1832.

My dear Bowles—

I deferred writing for a day or two from my plans being so uncertain, but it is now fixed that I go to London on Monday, which puts an end to all our visions of Music, Psalmody, Salisbury girls, &c, &c. I do not quite like being routed from home juſt now (except, indeed, for you and such articles as the above-mentioned) but business makes it necessary for me to visit " the City of the Plague," where I shall ſtay, for all reasons, as short a time as possible.

With beſt regards to Mrs. Bowles,
Yours ever moſt sincerely,
THOMAS MOORE.

Moore to Mrs. Bowles

Tuesday.

My dear Mrs. Bowles—

We should like (if you have no objection) to put off our visit to you, which Bowles fixed for Tuesday next, till some later period, when we might be able to combine with the pleasure of dining with you that of also hearing Bowles preach, which my sister has set her heart upon as one of the recollections she should like to carry back with her to Ireland. If I do not hear from you soon in answer to this, I shall take for granted that our engagement for Tuesday is given up.

Ever yours most truly,

THOMAS MOORE.

Moore to Bowles

My dear Bowles—

I am still too much of an invalid to come to Bath, and have been obliged to let Bessy go without me to-day. I hope she will be lucky enough to meet you and Mrs. Bowles.

I desired the Longmans to do what you wished, and also mentioned the offer of publication at their house, but they have not answered me. I take for granted, however, that the announcement has appeared, as they seldom are inattentive to any thing I request of them. What are you doing with respect to this?

You see Blackwood has laid on hard, but it is very well done—by far the cleverest thing yet written on the subject.

Yours, &c.,

T. MOORE.

Moore to Bowles

May 7, 1833.

My dear Bowles—

I was most sorry to have missed you on Saturday and, provokingly, I arrived at home about ten minutes after you were gone. I want much to see and hear how you are and how you have been and fared since we last met. Would that Sloperton and Bremhill could be thrown beside each other,—by any means but a convulsion of nature, which, God knows, we don't want just now, having plenty of convulsion, in the political way, preparing for us. But it is a sad thing that you and I, Arcades ambo, should be so far separated. My foot still prevents any effort of pedestrianism, but I should like a day with you at Bath prodigiously.

Best regards to Mrs. Bowles,

Ever yours truly,

T. MOORE.

Moore to Bowles

Tuesday.

My dear Bowles—

I forgot when Hughes gave me your note yesterday that the day was to be so soon. I am sorry to say I cannot go with you. I hate to be made sing at such a large party as the Anacreontic, and refusing is both disagreeable and troublesome.

I am delighted that Methuen and you have made up.[1] He should see your answer which was sensible and good-humoured and *firm* at the same time.

Yrs. ever,

T. MOORE.

[1] Paul Methuen, of Corsham, Wiltshire, had opposed Bowles in the Catherine Cook case.

Moore to Bowles

Friday.

My dear Bowles—

In coming home I read the article more atten-
tively, and feel perhaps that I was a little unjust, as
well as ungrateful, in the way I spoke of it.   There
are, I find, passages of a serious kind that show considerable powers of writing, and the author is no doubt
a very clever fellow; but he is one of those " *creatures
moving along Fancy's enchanted floor* " (to quote a
strange phrase of his own) that cut rather awkward
capers on said " floor," both in the way of *ground*
(grand ?) and *lofty* tumbling—both in declamation
and in humour; and I still think his fun of the very
worst quality possible.   The article, however, is a
good article, and a friendly article, and, if it will but
help the sale of *my* article, I shall be most exceedingly
obliged to it.

Yours ever,   T. M.

Moore to Bowles

My dear Bowles—

I quite forgot in the midst of our gaieties
yesterday to propose to you and Linley to come and
dine here on Friday next, which I most anxiously
hope you may be able to do; as it would be contrary
to all the rules of Anacreontic brotherhood that Linley
should again leave this neighbourhood without tasting
my Port. *If* you can come, pray send the inclosed to
Sir Guy Campbell, who perhaps will consent to meet
you.   Yours, my dear Bowles, very faithfully,

THOMAS MOORE.

You will understand that the note is not to go to
Sir Guy, unless you can come.   If you prefer Saturday,
it will be all the same to me—only let me have an
answer by bearer.   We shall dine at 5.

Moore to Bowles

Thursday, [November, 1836].

My dear Bowles—

I sent to [illegible] immediately on receiving your note, and finding that he goes to Bremhill on Monday and will take me and Tom, we shall both be most happy to come to you.

I never was much more pressed for time than just now, having had visitors in the house during the last fortnight who have played the very deuce with my lucubrations. The pleasure of meeting Southey however (and in *your house*) is not to be resisted.

Ever yours most truly,

Thomas Moore.

Sheridan to Bowles

April 10*th*, [1802 ?]

Dear Mr. Bowles,

I have spoken to Tom[1] who says you are too late for this year, as all the glees have been presented some time, but that for another year all you have to do is to send whatever you wish to be presented to Knyvett,[2] and it is certain of taking its fair chance. I am particularly disappointed at this, as I shall not now be at liberty to sing the glee which after all I *stole*, and which I think quite beautiful, but which upon my honor I have shewn to nobody, nor will I without your express permission. I am still at Fenton's Hotel, St. James St., consequently have not yet been able to make use of my dear Purcell.[3] When I do get settled, I will make up for time lost. Pray give my best regards to Mrs. Bowles, and believe me,
Yrs. very truly,
R. B. SHERIDAN.

---

[1] Probably Sheridan's son Tom.
[2] Charles Knyvett (1752–1822), musician. In 1801–02 he managed vocal concerts at the Hanover Square Rooms.
[3] Probably a gift from Bowles, who was fond of Purcell.

Sheridan to Bowles

CARLTON HOUSE, *October* 12*th*, [1804].

Dear Bowles [1]
     I received yours this morning being luckily
in town, as is also the Prince for a few days. I have
this moment seen him, and moſt graciously will he
receive your dedication. I certainly should wish you
to present your morocco yourself, but I muſt apprise
you of his motions. Upon your queſtion of the
manner of dedicating I will write a few lines to-morrow
or next day. You date only Donhead and I forget
whether it be your new or old residence,[2] but I will
enclose to John's.
                    [Signature cut from letter.]

---

[1] Directed to Bowles at Miss Costello's, Haymarket. Bowles's
dedication of *The Spirit of Discovery* to the Prince of Wales is dated
" Donhead, Nov. 3, 1804." Probably Bowles was introduced to the
Prince, for on the title-page of the volume he is described as " Chaplain
to His Royal Highness the Prince of Wales."

[2] Bowles had received the appointment to the vicarage of Bremhill,
but apparently was still resident at Donhead.

Rogers to Bowles

LONDON, *June* 10*th*, 1800.

My dear Sir,

I cannot tell you how I thank you for your kind invitation. Believe me, I shall accept it very gladly whenever it is in my power. One hour's conversation with you, where you now are, would be worth all I can ever see of you amid the smoke and ſtir of this dim spot. I think it very probable that I may once more visit Devonshire on the approach of winter and, in that case, I shall moſt certainly not forget what will be no small inducement to take the journey.—I breakfaſted this morning at Flaxman's[1] with poor Hayley who seems bowed to the earth in body and mind. I fear he will never recover from the loss of his son. He is leaving Eartham.

Adieu, and believe me to be ever

Moſt truly and respeƈtfully yours,

SAML. ROGERS.

Rogers to Bowles

[*July*, 1803 ?].

My dear Bowles

After some refleƈtion I think I had beſt send the volumes[2] to you. In a thing of such importance

---

[1] John Flaxman (1755–1826), sculptor and draughtsman. The son of the poet Hayley had been placed as a pupil with him.

[2] Probably to be used by Bowles in his work on the edition of Pope.

I muſt not hesitate and I know you will take care of them. I have heard the nightingale often in the day-time—and Aikin in his Calendar of Nature confirms luckily what I said. See month April—" Sings by day as well as by night only his voice is drowned in the multitude and hence the poets call him a *night-warbler*." Indeed Warton, with all his charms, was no observer, and had no accuracy in any thing.[1] You will bring these volumes back with you in the spring, for I cannot tell you how I value them.

> In Vol. 7th, p. 26. Note.—Wycherley's Poems.
> 217. Note he *shewed* them *indeed* with anger, but he found &c.
> 247 Note Grammont.
> 248 Do. Grammont.

These are all and are trifles but might have escaped you. Adieu. I am in all the misery of packing and the chaise is at the door. I shall leave the parcel with Cadell. Pray write a line to me at Keswick where I hope soon to be,[2] mentioning their safe arrival.

Ever, ever yours,

SAML. ROGERS.

I wish I deserved any mention of yours with the names you mention, but happy should I be to see our two names in conjunction at any time.

---

[1] The reference is to Joseph Warton, who had edited Pope.

[2] Rogers left London July 24, 1803, and passed through the Lake Country in early August. Coleridge was resident at Greta Hall, Keswick, 1800–03 ; and Southey began his residence under the same roof in 1803. Rogers, it appears, saw only Coleridge and Wordsworth.

Rogers to Bowles

Monday.

My dear Bowles

I am very, very sorry that we have not met. Can you breakfast with me to-morrow? If so, pray do and pray say you will—or *when* you can. I am just now at Holland House, but will come at a moment's notice, whenever I may have a chance of seeing you and I will let Moore know, who wishes much to meet you.

Ever yours,

SAML. ROGERS.

Rogers to Mrs. Bowles

My dear Mrs. Bowles

A thousand thanks for your present. I shall value it most highly on your account—not less than for its own sake and the author's. If I do not see you again, good bye—and pray, pray don't forget us in the spring.

[Signature cut from letter.]

Rogers to Mrs. Bowles

ST. JAMES'S PLACE, *Ap.* 30.

Dear Mrs. Bowles,

No. 18 Burlington St. is occupied, nor is there any first floor thereabouts. Jermyn Street I should think a good situation for you, particularly as being near Bury Street and the Baths—but had not you better come up to some quiet hotel and chuse for yourselves? Besides at this full season with the chance of letting any day, I apprehend nobody will

agree to let their lodging for so distant a time as the
11th of May. I am sorry to hear of the eruption but
am sure it is a subject for congratulation, not condo-
lence. My sister who is with me just now, desires to
be kindly remembered to you both.

Ever yours very truly,
SAML. ROGERS.

I will do whatever you direct with pleasure.

Rogers to Mrs. Bowles

BOWOOD, Tuesday.

My dear Mrs. Bowles
    Then after much negotiation and many per-
plexities it has been settled that we are to come to
you to-morrow and to accompany you both to Charlton
on Saturday. Lord Suffolk has a rent-feast on Friday,
at which he always presides. So, alas, we had no
alternative. Your Sabbath on the green[1] I have seen
and admired again and again and my sister is determined not to lose it, sooner or later. As to our man
and maid they are sure to be delighted under your
roof. A second table (what Bowles alluded to this
morning) they never knew under our own.

Yours ever,
SAML. ROGERS.

Rogers to Bowles

April 19, 1838.

My dear Friend
    A thousand thanks for your very welcome
letter—welcome indeed, for it told me that you were
both well after a winter that has swept away many I

---

[1] Bowles and Mrs. Bowles gave secular and religious instruction
at Bremhill to many poor children of the parish. The Marchioness of
Lansdowne was responsible for similar activities at Bowood.

H

could ill spare.   You say nothing of a journey east-
ward.   Salisbury has supplanted London in your
regard and we are never again, I fear, to see either
of you, unless we climb your hill.   My sister desires
to be very affectionately remembered to you both.   I
am Eastering at Strathfield Saye[1] and have asked an
old schoolfellow of yours to frank this letter, because
I knew it would give pleasure to him and to you.

Yours ever,
S. ROGERS.

Rogers to Mrs. Bowles

[1839].

My dear Mrs. Bowles

How ungrateful you must both have thought
me, so kind as your letters were and so welcome too.
I have seen the Collingwoods, (the mother, alas, on a
sofa) and have at once fallen in love with the young
lady.—I can only say that I have thought of you both,
morning, noon and nights, and this is the third frank
I have procured for the purpose of thanking you—
tho' I am half angry when I think of your long absence
from this town of ours—from Piccadilly now so gay
and from my nightingales now in full song.

Wordsworth is still here, delighted with the glimpse
he had of you both at Bath.   Pray tell Moore, when
you see him, to come before we break up.   Farewell,
my dear Mrs. Bowles, till we meet at Bremhill.

Yours ever and ever,
S. ROGERS.

My sister's best love to you both.

---

[1] An estate in Hampshire presented, in 1817, to the Duke of
Wellington.

Lord Lansdowne to Bowles

BOWOOD, *Sepr. 4th*, 1810.

My dear Sir

I shall not forget what you mention respecting Lane, whenever I have occasion to do any thing to the rock work at Bowood. At present there is so much essential repair wanted there, and I have also so much upon my hands in London, that I shall delay doing any thing that is not indispensible, till I am able to reside in Wiltshire, particularly in the ornamental department, which I can only judge of and direct upon the spot. I perfectly remember Lane who is an excellent executive workman, altho' if I am not mistaken, his haste (taste ?) requires sometimes the active superintendence of his employer, as you may perhaps have found at Bremhill. Your garden there is certainly one of the prettiest spots in the county.

I expect our friend [illegible] here in a few days. He has suffered a severe blow in the loss of his wife, and I am afraid his spirits are not yet recovered from the shock.

I remain, my dear sir, with sincere regard,
Your faithful servant,
LANSDOWNE.

Lord Lansdowne to Bowles

LONDON, *Jany.* 25*th*, [1813].

My dear Sir [1]

Many thanks for your letter. Your absence from Wiltshire is unfortunate at such a moment, but I hope we may prevail upon you to accompany the D. of Somerset, Lord Holland, [and] myself from Reading, as we shall have a place for you, and can with perfect convenience bring you back to Reading on our return; and really your countenance and presence, particularly as Mr. Douglas and Mr. A [illegible] will be absent, is important to the cause of liberality and common sense, and we shall be lucky in the pleasure of your company.

Yours most truly,
LANSDOWNE.

We shall stop at the Evans Inn, and be there between twelve and one o'clock.

Lord Lansdowne to Bowles

BOWOOD, *Tuesday*, [*October*, 1813].

My dear Sir

I think you have expressed some curiosity to see Madame de Staël.

Will you come and dine with her Friday ?[2]   We can give you a bed if you like it.

Yrs. truly,
LANSDOWNE.

[1] Letter directed to the house of Archdeacon Nares, Reading.
[2] " In riding to Bowood," wrote Maria Edgeworth in 1818, " he fell, and sprained his shoulder, but still came on. Lord Lansdowne alluded to this in presenting him to Madame de Staël before dinner in the midst of the listening circle. She began to compliment him and

Lady Lansdowne to Mrs. Bowles

[BOWOOD, *Oct.*, 1813 ?].

My dear Mrs. Bowles

I am very sorry indeed to find that your foot still gives you so much pain. I am sure that such a confinement must be particularly irksome to you. I am sorry not to have been able to pay you a visit and inquire after you but we have had so large a party in the house that I have not been my own mistress. Mr. Rogers left us yesterday. He charged me with his farewell to you and his regrets that my having carried him off to [illegible] prevented his having had the pleasure of walking over to bid you goodbye on Wednesday as he had intended.

Can you give me any intelligence about the harvest that we may settle the holydays? She asked me yesterday and I said that I would let her know Monday. I hope to see you still at Salisbury. It is so very tranquil an entertainment I think you may venture and I should not mind a stich if I were you.

Very sinly. yrs.,

L. LANSDOWNE.

We are going to show Bath to our foreign friends to-day.

Have you received your gown?

herself upon the exertion he had made to come and see her : ' Oh, ma'am, say no more, for I would have done a great deal more to see so great a curiosity !' Lord Lansdowne says it is impossible to describe the *shock* in Madame de Staël's face—the breathless astonishment and the total change produced in her opinion of the man. She afterwards said to Lord Lansdowne, who had told her he was a simple country clergyman, ' Je vois bien que ce n'st qu'un simple curé qui n'a pas le sens commun, quoique grand poète.' "

Madame de Staël to Bowles

Monday, [*Oct.,* 1813].

Thousand thanks for your kindness, my dear sir. If I hear an anthem, I'll pray for you. Poetry and religion are re-united in you, as they muſt be always.[1] My beſt compliments to Mrs. Bowles.

I am yours,

[Illegible] Necker, &c.

STAËL HOLSTEIN.

I came back from Bath. It is a very magnificent town.

Lord Lansdowne to Bowles

BOWOOD, *August 2d,* 1814.

My dear Sir

I have juſt had some imitations made of the beſt form of Etruscan vases in the Museum for the library here, and as they have succeeded entirely and are very perfeét imitations of the originals, I will beg your acceptance of one of them in the hope that you will for my sake find a corner for it in your parsonage.

I beg my compliments to Mrs. Bowles. We are juſt setting out for Dorsetshire.

Yours very truly,

LANSDOWNE.

---

[1] She admired the *Sonnets* and *The Spirit of Discovery,* and translated the " Hotwells Elegy " into French.

Lady Lansdowne to Mrs. Bowles

Thursday, [*March,* 1815; LONDON].

Dear Mrs. Bowles

I am very happy to find that success has crowned your labors and that a woman has been found to chaperonne Anne. I have desired Mrs. Broad to write by to-day's post to the woman who has the charge of the furniture which was prepared for the school house to have it sent there immediately and also to desire Savory (?) to pay her weekly as you recommended—and as I conclude her wardrobe is not very rich, I must beg you will order what will make her look decent and give a sufficient change of linen, and desire it to be placed to my account at Calne.

I wish in return for all this trouble I could send you some good news but nothing can be more gloomy than all we hear. War, eternal war, I fear, is to be our portion, and we are told that nothing but positive inability to wage it, can give us peace. We do not know what to hope !

Poor Madame de Staël was within *two hours* of receiving the money the French Government owed her and which was destined as her daughter's marriage portion, the Duc de Broglie being too poor to marry without it, so both their prospects have vanished by Bonaparte's appearance.[1]

Lord L. desires his best compliments to you and Mr. Bowles. We have been enjoying the last two fine days in the country which was the reason I did not answer your letter yesterday and I quite forgot

---

[1] Napoleon landed in France March 1, 1815. Madame de Staël's daughter married the Duc de Broglie in February, 1816.

when I wrote laſt to say how entirely I approved your
suggeſtion about the children's holydays at harveſt
time.   Moſt sincerely your obliged,
                                   LOUISA LANSDOWNE.

Lady Lansdowne to Mrs. Bowles

[LONDON (?)], *March* 23*d*, [1815].

My dear Madam
        I am very much obliged to you for your two
letters.   It is impossible for me to express my satisfaction at the school's having gone on so well during
my absence.   I think it has been a great trial for the
miſtress and as she has ſtood it, I think she has proved
that she may be depended upon.   I quite agree with
you that if we could get a person to have in the school
it would be a thousand times better than removing
Anne, but it really appears so hopeless that I am in
despair about it, and the letter Mrs. Savory (?) wrote
to Mrs. Broad was so very urgent to have Anne removed, that I thought she really would not keep her
a week longer, which made me think of our conversation about the widow.
        I am quite grieved at having missed the woman
you mention.   I had never heard of her before.   Do
you think it would be practicable to get a person for
a year or less ?   It might be an accommodation to
some one in that way and would give us time to look
about.   But I requeſt that you will settle whatever
you think the beſt as I am sure you are much the
beſt judge and that I shall approve of whatever you
determine.
        The public news is so very gloomy that it is painful
to dwell upon it.   The beginning of another twenty
years of war and misery is an awful prospect and I
fear there is no chance of any thing else.

We are very glad that you have begun an acquaintance with Mr. Crabbe. We were afraid that he intended to shut himself up in the delights of Trowbridge. With Lord L's best compliments, I remain

Moſt sinly. yr. obliged

L. LANSDOWNE.

Lady Lansdowne to Mrs. Bowles

[LONDON, 1816].

My dear Madam

I have been a very long time thanking you for your laſt kind letter but I am sure that you will forgive me when you hear the reason, which has been the serious illness of all my children. The poor little baby was so ill for several days that I was very much alarmed about him. They are now recovering but till spring weather comes I cannot hope to see them quite well.—I enclose you a copy of Lord Byron's farewell to Lady Byron which he sent to her the day after their separation was signed. In spite of one's self it is impossible not to feel for him while one reads it, tho I believe firmly that he felt nothing whilſt he wrote it, and his sending it to Murray the bookseller with leave to show it, is a pretty good proof of it. I believe Ly. B. endured as much as was possible without complaining but I fear she has too ſtrong feelings ever to be happy again.

This has been the moſt unhealthy season in London known for many years. There have not been so many deaths in the same time since the time of the great plague. There are great differences of opinion about Miss O'Neil's success in comedy but I think the majority agree in thinking she has not lightness and ease sufficient for Lady Teazle.[1] Have you seen Mr.

---

[1] Miss O'Neill was extraordinarily successful in London from 1814 to 1819. She was best in tragic parts. With her marriage in 1819 she retired from the stage.

Hobhouse's " Substance of Letters written from Paris in 1815 "? His name is not to it, but he allows it to have been written by himself. It is very interesting and written with so—— [Rest of letter missing.]

Lord Lansdowne to Bowles

BOWOOD, *Friday.*

My dear Sir

I am ready for an expedition to Trowbridge to-morrow, but if it is as hot as I found it to-day coming from Longleat,[1] I am afraid we should find it rather too long a ride to be pleasant, in these dog days. Perhaps however you will come over to break-fast, and if you do I will take *a* ride with you at all events if we should find it too hot to proceed.

I should have written before if we had not staid at Longleat longer than we intended.

Will you give us the pleasure of your company to dinner on Monday the 31st?

Yours very sincerely,
LANSDOWNE.

Lady Lansdowne to Mrs. Bowles

[LONDON, 1818].

My dear Mrs. Bowles

I am very much obliged to you for your com-munication about Anne. She is determined to lessen our regrets at losing her by persevering in her artful line of conduct to the end. It is extremely kind of you to intend remaining at home to receive our new mistress. Her beginning well is of so much conse-quence to her future good conduct that I feel quite

---

[1] Seat of the Marquis of Bath.

confident, as you so kindly undertake setting her off, in her final success.

We have the worst weather I ever remember in London. The fogs are so thick that at night it is quite difficult to go about the streets, and by day in the house it is by the light alone of the fire we can see to do any thing.

Miss O'Neil, I hear, acts most beautifully in Bianca, but Fazio is not expected to have a great run.[1] The Bride of Abydos is thought very bad.[2] . . .

We have had a sad loss in Lord Lansdowne's uncle Lord Kerry (?) who was very fond of him and who enjoyed such good health that we looked forward to many years more of enjoyment for him and comfort to ourselves in his society. . . .

[Last part of letter missing.]

Lady Lansdowne to Mrs. Bowles

[LONDON (?)].

My dear Mrs. Bowles

I am very sorry to hear that you have been so unwell. I hope that you have had some other advice than Calne affords, as I do not think that is very good at present. Lord L. desires me to say with his best compliments that he strongly recommends your crossing the plain to consult Dr. Fowler, which in his opinion would be having the best advice the country affords not excepting London. I must recommend for my part your trying the yolk of a raw egg beat up with sugar and either milk or wine once or twice a day. I have found it answer when nothing else agreed with my stomach.

---

[1] *Fazio*, by H. H. Milman, was published in 1815, but first acted in London, February 5, 1818, with Miss O'Neill as Bianca.

[2] A play by William Dimond based upon *The Bride of Abydos* was given at Drury Lane 14 times in the season 1817–18.

With respect to the [illegible], I cannot take in the little girl for she is not six and I shall not break thro' any rules for them. It is a great pity about Anne for she will soon forget the little she has learnt.

I hope to hear soon that you are better and should be much obliged to you if you will give me a line to tell me how you are. Lord L. is nearly well. We are going into Surrey for change of air for a few days.

Very sinly. yrs.,

L. LANSDOWNE.

Pray give our best compliments to Mr. Bowles.

Lady Lansdowne to Mrs. Bowles

[BOWOOD] *Saty.*

My dear Mrs. Bowles

It is too bad to plague you so soon about parish matters, but there is no doing without you. I hear such contradictory accounts of Mary Britton's daughter I am quite puzzled what to do. Isaac Britton and his wife whom I asked separately the same day, so they could not concert together, said she was reformed and they had heard nothing against her for five or six years, and yesterday I was told from another quarter that she spent her Sunday nights at the ale house and the rest of her conduct was of that cast. Now if this is true it must be known, as all frequenters of the ale house must see her. Could you have some inquiry made for me? as if it turns out to be so I must not admit her as my lodger.

Pray let me know when you want any other book to amuse you.

Yrs. very sinly.,

L. LANSDOWNE.

I hope you keep yourself very warm.

Lady Lansdowne to Mrs. Bowles

My dear Mrs. Bowles   [LONDON,] *Saty.*

    Will you be so kind when you go again to the school to tell Mrs. P. that I truſt for the future she will give no cause for busy tongues and that I hope the school will continue to prosper under her care (which it certainly has done). I am unwilling to write myself to her as I think it is difficult to word it so as not either to make her consider it as a complete acquittal or as a censure, which I am willing to suspend.

    Our servants believe Mead has proposed but that all his family were so violently againſt it, he gave it up—and I dare say they have made the moſt of any reports they could pick up to her disadvantage.

    I am much obliged to you for all the trouble you have taken in this business.

    You will have been, I am sure, very much shocked at Sir J. Macdonald's death. He was quite well on Wednesday and on Thursday evening was doing business with his secretary when he was taken so ill that in a very short time his case was hopeless.

    .   .   .   .

    Pray remember us moſt kindly to Mr. Bowles. Charles Fox is going to ſtand for Shaftesbury. I hope Mr. B.'s brother will befriend him.

Ever yrs.,
L. L.

Lady Lansdowne to Mrs. Bowles

Dear Madam   [LONDON].

    I am extremely obliged to you for the account of our new miſtress which is more satisfactory than I had dared to hope for. The Catechisms are on their

road and I hope will soon arrive. I quite agree with
you about the regulation of two years' stay in the
school, but I fear without we contrive some forfeit
or give some great reward, which perhaps would be
the easiest, our regulation would be of no use as the
promise, I am afraid, would not be very binding to
the parents if their children could earn any thing.

I am quite surprised to hear of Mr. Bowles's
spirited intentions. I hope he will keep to them as I
think you will have much pleasure in your tour. As
for him I think the pleasures and pains will be so
nicely balanced that I do not know which will prevail.
I have had one visit from Mrs. Dart (?). She lives
in *Camomile* (?), not a very poetic residence. She has
above 300 subscribers and is in great spirits and will,
I fear, become in the end disagreeable beyond measure.
I am sure in idea she considers herself upon a level
with the first poets of the age and talks with great
pleasure of the apprehended severity of the Edinburgh
Review. If her poems have any success she has very
great ulterior views ! But I fancy she will end at once.

Lord L. has had a very bad cold and the children
do nothing but cough. The alternate cold and heat
has made London quite an hospital.

I look forward with much pleasure to seeing you
soon in town, and depend upon your letting me know
when you arrive. Lord L. desires his best compliments to you and Mr. B., and believe me ever,

Sinly. yrs. &c.,
L. L.

Lady Lansdowne to Mrs. Bowles

[Bowood.]

My dear Mrs. Bowles
I have seen a person whom I think would suit
us as a schoolmistress. She is a friend of Marianne's

(our workwoman) who has known her for some time. She has for the last year been schoolmistress at Chippenham but finds the salary so small she wishes to leave it, tho' if I do not take her she will be glad to remain there and wishes nothing to be said about it. She is a widow between forty and fifty with a steady and rather stiff decided manner which I am sure would suit the children much better than Mrs. White's dandling ways and she looks as if she would comprehend what one said to her, which Mrs. White does not. She can teach the four first rules in arithmetic and has taught all the rest of our arts at Chippenham to girls but does not object to boys. I told her I would consult with you and let her know in the course of a week as I could not do any thing without your advice. She could not come before Lady Day as she must give them notice at Chippenham and I told her I should give Mrs. White three months' notice before I parted from her. If you are likely to be at the school on Monday I could meet you there or will send the [illegible], as you like best, to talk this over. On Tuesday we go to Lord Suffolks for two days.

Very sinly. yrs.,
L. L.

Her name is Henly. She has no children or they are disposed of.

Lady Lansdowne to Mrs. Bowles

[BOWOOD].

My dear Madam—
I am extremely sorry that the office you so kindly undertook of sending for a school mistress has given you so much trouble as I fear it must have done and I feel quite ashamed of being able to do nothing to assist you at present. I should think that person

must understand the working part as far as settling the work for the children, as otherwise that would take up too much of our little teacher's time.

We are quite delighted with the Little Hymn Book.[1]   The simplicity and beauty of the compositions quite charm us, and I am sure they will be very popular amongst our children.   It is quite admirable of Mr. Bowles to lower his Muse in so kind a manner, to adapt it to such early readers.

I beg you will send to Bowood for as many fish as you wish to have.   I am extremely happy to be able to contribute a *mite* to the bounty of Bremhill.

Lord L. unites with me in best compliments to you and Mr. Bowles and many thanks for all the assistance you are giving us.

Most sinly. yrs. &c.,
LOUISA LANSDOWNE.

Lady Lansdowne to Mrs. Bowles

BERK[ELEY SQUARE, LONDON].

My dear Mrs. Bowles
        I was very glad to hear of your safe return to dear Bremhill.[2]   Of your warm reception there could be no doubt.   There is always so many lamentations at your absence, and such a blank is felt in all the neighborhood when you cross the plain.

I am very sorry for Mrs. Bridgman's alarm and I hope her nerves will recover, but as there has been a school there so many years without any alarm and nothing was taken I think she may remain satisfied with some additional fastenings, as I am not inclined to spoil the room by putting up a partition.   If she

---

[1] *The Little Villager's Verse Book*, possibly in one of its earlier issues.

[2] After the three winter months at Salisbury.

chuses to have a male protector she can let him go to bed first and get up before him. I dare say that she will think me very hard-hearted, but I have not very great sympathy with her fears.

Our evergreens here are all nearly killed. Some very fine ilex's which were the pride of the garden are so sick I fear they cannot recover. It alters the whole look of the place in a very dismal manner and makes me tremble for the pleasure ground at Bowood. I hope Maude Heath[1] looks well and that you approve her head-dress. It cost a great deal of research to get it correctly designed.

. . . .

Pray remember us to Mr. B. and believe me ever
Yrs. most sinly.,
L. L.

Lady Lansdowne to Mrs. Bowles

[LONDON].

My dear Mrs. Bowles

I was very glad to receive a letter from you dated from your dear Bremhill, as I well know all the enjoyment that you have there, and now that the weather has become more spring-like it must be quite delightful. We had some very charming music last night for the Queen who enjoyed it very much. I enclose you a programme that you may see what we had. It may perhaps amuse Mr. Bowles. The novelty of going to another person's house amused the Queen and she was apparently very much entertained.

I am a good deal tired to-day but am so much stronger than I was last year that I shall soon recover it.

I hope you will soon see the Foxham School as a

[1] Maud Heath was a public-spirited peasant-woman of Wiltshire in mediæval times. Bowles and Lansdowne erected a monument to her.

little encouragement from you will do the miſtress much good, as she is new to responsibility and amongſt ſtrangers muſt feel forlorn.

Mr. Rogers is much better this year, less deaf and more disposed to be pleased. Miss Rogers I have not seen.

Lord L. has had a tedious set of the gout, but now he has got upon his horse again I truſt his foot will soon get ſtrong. Son is very flourishing. Pray remember us particularly to Mr. Bowles and believe me ever moſt

Sinly. yrs.,

L. LANSDOWNE.

The Bowles-Byron Controversy

Southey to Bowles

[1819].

My dear Sir

I thank you for your letter to Campbell.[1] I
saw in a newspaper the passage which provoked it,
and thought it very feeble and very shallow; but I
had no suspicion that it was founded upon so gross a
misstatement as that which you have proved, and
probably accounted for. Thus it is that reviews, the
most unfaithful of all writings, are the only ones
which are taken implicitly upon trust.[2] It is needless
to add that I agree with you entirely upon the invariable principles of poetry: we learned them in the

[1] Bowles, invited by a syndicate of publishers to edit Pope's works,
brought out in 1806 a 10-volume edition. This was adversely noticed
in the *Edinburgh Review* in January, 1808. The following year Byron,
who was familiar with the *Edinburgh* article, satirized Bowles in the
first and second editions of *English Bards and Scotch Reviewers*. Bowles,
in an interview with Byron at the house of Rogers in 1812, pointed
out certain misrepresentations in the satire, due to too implicit reliance
upon statements made in the *Edinburgh*. Byron admitted his error, and
for a long period thereafter Bowles underwent no further censure from
prominent quarters. He was subjected, however, to intermittent
criticism, often of a casual nature, from writers of small consequence.
Early in 1819 Thomas Campbell issued, in 7 volumes, his *Specimens
of the British Poets*. In this he attacked the edition of Pope, particularly the principles by which Pope's poetry was judged. Bowles, feeling that the time had come for him to defend himself, replied in April
of the same year with his *Invariable Principles of Poetry*. Campbell
was silent, and the controversy would probably have ended here had
not the publication of Spence's *Anecdotes* in 1820 brought Pope's rank
and personal character once more under discussion.

[2] Bowles taxed Campbell, perhaps justly, with deriving his ideas
of the edition of Pope from the *Edinburgh* article.

same school, and I was confirmed in them in my youth by seeing them exemplified in your writings.

It would have given me great pleasure if I could have met you at General Peachy's. My intended movements were delayed by the growth of an enormous volume under my hands, the extent whereof it was impossible to calculate, because no one had ever travelled the ground before me: and the materials lay scattered far and wide, so that their amount could never be known till they were brought together. However I am printing the laſt chapter, and shall in a few weeks have the satisfaction of completing a great hiſtorical work, on which I might be well content to reſt my hopes of a laſting reputation.

I was much pleased and affected by your account of the poor woman and the "cruel Calviniſt"[1] which Peachy put into my hands. That ſtory ought to be widely circulated as a warning and an example. I spoke of it in a paper printed for the Quarterly Review six months ago, but ſtill, I know not for what reason, laid aside. I look upon Calvinism as the worſt corruption of Chriſtianity; there is nothing in Popery itself so likely to produce corruption of morals and hardness of heart, if it were followed to its legitimate consequences;—and nothing so monſtrous as its doctrine, in the moſt revolting mythology that was ever imposed upon poor human credulity. I love Wesley for the irresiſtible ſtrength of reasoning and of feeling with which he opposed it: yet so widely is it diffused and so bitter is its spirit, that this opposition brought upon him more obloquy tenfold, than any other part of his conduct, obnoxious as it sometimes was to censure.

Farewell, my dear sir, and believe me
Yours with sincere respect,
ROBERT SOUTHEY.

[1] A pamphlet which Bowles issued about this time.

Bowles to Thomas Campbell

BREMHILL, *April* 18*th*, 1819.

[My dear Sir] [1]

I have thought myself called upon to vindicate some observations of mine on the character of Pope, in answer to your critical remarks on those observations in the 1st volume of your Specimens. I think you have hastily laid yourself open to some animadversions; but I trust you will find nothing said that might seem to imply any feelings but those of the highest respect for your acknowledged political and literary character. Your friend Moore is in this neighbourhood, as also Crabbe and Crewe. It would give me great pleasure if I should ever have an opportunity of seeing you here; and believe me that, though our aspects are somewhat warlike in *print*, at *home* I remain most sincerely and faithfully, and with many thanks for the great pleasure I have derived from your works,

Your most obedient servant,

W. L. BOWLES.

Thomas Campbell to Bowles

SYDENHAM, KENT, *April* 18, 1819.

Dear Sir

I received your agreeable letter this morning and I shall regard myself as at least of some use to literature if the very defects of my critical reasonings can again draw forth the pen of Mr. Bowles. I have no doubt that your powers of illustration will make a

---

[1] The letter is reprinted by permission from William Beattie's *Life and Letters of Thomas Campbell*, Vol. II, page 349.

strong case out of the opinions which you support and I trust that you will not find me an uncandid antagonist making bare allowance for that sentiment which Dr. Sangrado addressed to his medical pupil: " My dear Gil Blas, how can you expect a man to change his opinion when he has written a book to support it ? " Whatever I may have to fear from the intrinsic force of your animadversions I have from the refinement of your character the most perfect confidence of being used by you in a gentlemanlike manner. I can sincerely assure you that I have long anticipated your wish that we should be better acquainted. This sentiment I think my friends Moore and Crabbe must remember to have heard me warmly express when they delighted me with a visit to Sydenham and when we mentioned your name and wished for your presence. If chance should bring you to London and if you can spare the time and the trouble you will confer an honour and a pleasure that I shall sensibly feel by spending a day under my humble roof.

Believe me, dear Sir,

With respect and admiration,

Yours truly,

T. CAMPBELL.

" *Christopher North* " *to Bowles*

EDIN[BURGH], 21 *July*, 1819.

The Editor of Blackwood's Magazine[1] takes the liberty of sending to Mr. Bowles the last number of that work, in the hope that Mr. Bowles will be of opinion that justice has been done him in the account

---

[1] The actual writer was perhaps William Blackwood, but the letter was almost certainly inspired by " Christopher North," Bowles's friend.

of his controversy with his distinguished brother-poet
Mr. Campbell.[1]

The Editor cannot suppose that Mr. Bowles, in
the midst of far more important avocations, would
trouble himself with writing any thing for this work,
but if he thinks that any of his younger friends might
do so, the Editor would consider himself indebted to
Mr. Bowles for any such communication.   He ventures to say this much in the hope that, though Blackwood's Magazine, like all other miscellaneous works,
may have contained opinions and feelings with which
Mr. Bowles may not have sympathized, the general
tone of that work has been favourable to the cause of
taste, morality, and religion.

Southey to Bowles

KESWICK, 16 *Oct.*, 1820.

My dear Sir
          I was so much hurt and offended by the manner
in which you are treated in the last Quarterly Review[2]
that my first impulse was to have written to you and
expressed my indignation.   Indeed the general temper
of that Journal in its criticism is as bad as that of the
Edinburgh Review, and its principles in fine literature
not a whit better,—if principles they can be called,
being always arbitrary, frequently contradictory, and
sometimes nonsensical.   And I have so often been
disgusted by it that I should long ago have withdrawn

---

[1] *Blackwood's Magazine* in July, 1819, reviewed Bowles's *Invariable Principles of Poetry*. The writer held that Bowles could no longer
remain silent when assailed by a man of Campbell's standing, and that
he had successfully repelled every accusation brought against him.

[2] Isaac Disraeli (father of Benjamin Disraeli) contributed to the
Quarterly Review for July, 1820, an anonymous article on Spence's
Anecdotes. He handled Bowles's edition of Pope very roughly.

from the review, if it had been possible for me to have
acted upon the public mind with equal effect thro any
other medium.

You are quite at liberty to make use of any thing in
my letter which may suit your purpose.—Do not be
hasty in your reply; but make the most of a good
case, and you will put the Review to shame.   And
you should be *certain* that Gilchrist is the writer,[1]
before you make the remotest allusion to him.   I
never heard him mentioned as having contributed
any thing to the Quarterly Review.   But I have no
suspicion who the writer is.

If you were to pick out the contradictory opinions
upon poetry which have been at different times
expressed in this Journal, and arrange them in
parallel columns, they would make an amusing
harmony.   In the 23rd number, pp. 85–7, you will
see what I have said of Pope's Homer.   I should very
much like to show you the passage as it stood before
Mr. Gifford thought proper, not only to mutilate it,
but to interpolate it most unwarrantably with qualify-
ing expressions, for the purpose of taking away its
force.   Yet I was less hurt by this editorial interference,
injudicious and injurious as it was, than by the omission of a few words in a subsequent passage wherein
I had mentioned your name.   The words which I
had written and which the Editor thought proper to
expunge are inserted in my own copy, and it would
oblige me if Mrs. Bowles would insert them in yours,
—for which purpose I will copy part of the sentence
here and underline them (p. 89).—" Bowles who yet
lives *to enjoy his well-deserved reputation*, and to whom
we gladly *and gratefully* offer our thanks for the pleasure

---

[1] Unfortunately Bowles did not heed this advice.   He was led by
some diatribes against his *Pope* which Gilchrist had contributed to the
London Magazine, to impute the authorship of the *Quarterly* article to
Gilchrist.   This complicated the controversy, which had now become
bitterly and coarsely personal.

and benefit which we derived from his poems in our younger days."

If you were to see the manner in which Gifford has mutilated every paper of mine which has paſt thro his hands, you would marvel at my patience. But in truth I am weary of remonſtrating with him; whenever I have complained he has apologized and promised that he will make no alteration in future without my consent and approbation,—and in the next number he is at the same work again.

You are right to answer the Reviewer, because tho he will find more readers at present, you will be read hereafter when reviews and reviewers are forgotten. But you will not be right, if you suffer yourself to be vexed by an unhandsome and unfair attack, the futility of which must be perceived by all who underſtand the subjeƈt, and the manner of which muſt displease all who know you.

I dined with General Peachy yeſterday, and found your letter on my return. He would desire his remembrances if he knew I were writing to you. Friday next he sets off for—Glasgow and Edinburgh on his way to London, and Heaven knows where.

> Believe me, my dear sir,
> Yrs. very truly,
> ROBERT SOUTHEY.

Bowles to Murray

BREMHILL, *October* 22, 1820.

Dear Sir[1]   ungentlemanly
    After the ſtupid, ~~blackguard,~~ ~~and lying~~ article in the laſt Quarterly, deſtitute of even truth, so personally insulting to me, and as remote from sense as from manners, I am sure you will excuse a

---

[1] Murray was of course proprietor of the *Quarterly*.

good-natur'd " badinage " in which your name is
mention'd, but without the slightest disrespect.

Without those feelings that often excite, *as they
did in Pope*, vindictive asperity, I call the article
stupid, for the sophistry would not deceive a child;
I call it ~~blackguard,~~ ^{ungentlemanly} because no gentleman ever
us'd such insulting language to another; and I
call it ~~lying,~~ ^{destitute of even truth} because it says I have endeavour'd to
surmise away every amiable quality of Pope, which is
false ! and the writer knew it to be so !

If these were my solitary opinions I should have
too much pride to utter them, but I will venture to
say they are the opinions of nine-tenths of the readers
of the Quarterly who understand the subject spoken of,
and among many other letters I have received from
characters of the greatest distinction in literature, I
might mention the most decisive one of the best
reviewer that ever supported the Quarterly Review.

You will guess what impression, not against me,
but for me, the article has made when I transcribe a
word or two from Mr. Southey.

" I was so much hurt and offended by the manner
in which you are treated in the last Quarterly Review,
that my first impulse was to write to you and express
my indignation !

" You will be right to answer the reviewer, but you
will not be right if you suffer yourself to be vexed by
an unhandsome and unfair attack.   Its futility must
be perceived by all who understand the subject, and
the manner of which must displease all who know
you."

I merely transcribe these words to shew you that
what I have said is supported by authority which even
the Quarterly Review must respect.

I shall answer the whole, with my own name, and
do not fear to twist the author round my little finger,

and make those interested in the success of the Review ashamed they admitted such paltry arguments and such disgraceful personal spite to a man who never offended them.

In the mean time, a small publication which has been sent to me I send to you, and as I cannot suppose you have anything to do with the rejection or admission of most of the articles, I hope I may trust your kindness, I might say justice, to grant me one request. It is to place on your table the accompanying small publication.[1]   At all events I have no reason to complain of yourself, and I am, dear sir,

Very truly,
W. L. BOWLES.

If you look at what is said in the Review concerning " Rural Editors getting mad over Old Dunces," you will know what I mean by blackguardism.

The same author wrote in the London Review, and attacked me with the same flippancy, ignorance, affectation, and stupidity, but the editor wrote me a manly and generous letter totally disclaiming any participation in the sentiments and accounting for the admission by illness.[2]   That such a writer (for Nature never made two such in one age) should have been permitted [to] disgrace the Quarterly is a matter, not of exultation to me, but regret.

---

[1] The pamphlet was in reality an anonymous one by Bowles himself. Bowles's rather naive request to Murray produced a good deal of amusement among his friends.

[2] Bowles later repeated and expanded this statement in one of his pamphlets (without first obtaining permission), and mentioned the editor, John Scott, by name. Scott was deeply offended. He complained to his friends that Bowles had cited " private civilities as public testimonies," and had misrepresented his letter by suppressing one whole side of it. He admitted, however, what Bowles here states. The rights and wrongs of the question were still unsettled when Scott was killed in a duel.

Murray to Bowles

LONDON, *Octr.* 26, 1820.

Dear Sir

I received safely your obliging letter and the pamphlet which accompanied it. You are right in supposing that I have nothing to do with the communication to the Quarterly Review, and you do me but justice in believing that I shall readily place the pamphlet on my table to be read by every person who pleases. Indeed by referring to the last number of the Quarterly Review you will find that I have appended to it a reply to an article on Stephens' Thesaurus.

Your friend should not have stiled mine a *Reading-Room*, which it is not, in any sense, for it implies some kind of subscription or compensation, but the fact is, simply, that I open my drawing room for a few hours in the day time, instead of the evening, to the higher class of men of letters.

I am, with great esteem,
Dear sir,
Your obliged servant,
JOHN MURRAY.

Bowles to Murray

BREMHILL, *April 6th*, 1821.

My dear Sir[1]

I write once more to say I have just got Lord Byron's pamphlet, and I could not omit requesting you to return him my best thanks for the kind terms

---

[1] Byron, devoted to Pope, and fond of excitement, was anxious to embroil himself in the controversy. Several references to his name gave him a pretext. In March, 1821, he published his *Letter to* ****

in which he introduces my name, and also for the pleasure I have receiv'd from a work as much mark'd by good sense, liberal principles, and just thinking as by its peculiar tone of good-humour and urbanity, to which I have been of late so little accustom'd. He has hardly, I think, done justice to my estimation of Pope's poetry. If you will turn to what I have said, in the tenth volume, you will see I have in the Pathetic (speaking of the unrival'd Eloisa) placed him (so far from wishing to depreciate) above all writers in the same walk, both ancient and modern. I have said the same of his inimitable Rape of the Lock. I have in other parts said as much of his Ethic Epistles, his Essay on Criticism, [and] his Satires, preferring them to Juvenal or Horace; but Lord Byron, nor all the world, will ever convince me that in the " sublimity " of the Ode he is equal to Dryden, in descriptive poetry to Thomson or Cowper, or generally to Shakespeare or Milton.

These are my views of his poetry, from which I have never varied, and I am sure Lord Byron will think the same, and will believe I have not intended ever to depreciate his poetry, but merely to ascertain his rank, indubitably the highest in all he executed.

It is hard after such explicit statements to be told that I have affected to consider him " no great poet."

Lord Byron is the first liberal, manly, and kind-

****** [*John Murray*]. Though illogical, it possesses a verve which, together with the author's reputation, caused it to focus public attention on the discussion. Towards Bowles it is somewhat contemptuous in tone, though not violent or very coarse. Against Bowles's contention that images drawn from what is sublime or beautiful in nature are superior to any images drawn from art, it upholds the theory that it is the poet's powers of execution that count. " Mr. Bowles," says Byron, " makes the chief part of a ship's poesy depend upon the ' wind ' : then why is a ship under sail more poetical than a hog in a high wind ? The hog is all nature, the ship is all art, ... and yet nothing but excess of hunger could make me look upon a pig as the more poetical of the two, and then only in the shape of a griskin."

hearted opponent I have ever met,[1] and I feel even gratitude towards him, as much as I respect him, for the manly vindication, without asperity or unkindness, of Pope's moral character. It has weigh'd with me more than any thing I have ever read, particularly with regard to Pope's connection with Martha Blount.

In the principles of poetical criticism I shall think myself invulnerable, even from the polish'd lance of such an opponent. I knew he would mistake one point. I never spoke of Nature *as generally* more poetical than art, but that images from what is " sublime or beautiful " in Nature were so.

A pig in a high wind is natural enough, but not as a " sublime or beautiful " image in Nature, and of this only did I speak in my definition. I had examined long before, the most of Lord Byron's examples from the sublime of art, particularly sculpture, painting, &c., and I feel convinc'd that the exquisite description of his own Dying Gladiator will shew that his poetry will confirm my principles, tho this criticism opposes them.

I shall probably have to discuss these points further with him. He has set me an example of urbanity which I am sure will never be infring'd by me, and if I enter into further explanation and discussion with him on this subject, it will be for sake of truth, not victory.

When you write, give [him] my kind compliments and do not fail to say, if you have sent the last pamphlet, that this pamphlet has not yet been publish'd, owing to poor Scott's death, and that in deference to Lord Byron's opinions, of the justice of which I am now convinc'd, some passages which bear more immediately on Pope's moral character will be expung'd before it is advertised for sale. I only ask for truth and justice, not favour, and in your next edition [of Pope] I trust the editor will not impute motives, or

---

[1] Elsewhere Bowles adds Campbell's name to Byron's.

decry opinions, till he knows what those opinions really are.

It is most unfortunate that the words " Christian " community should have occurred so often in my last, but after I knew Mr. D'Israeli was the writer of the Quarterly, I solemnly declare I did not know his religious creed was so opposite from my own.

Lord Byron little knows who it is to whom he has given " Midas's ears " ![1]   I am speaking of the note in which it is said, " You have hit Pope in the head." What can Lord Byron allude to when he speaks of some story of my life ?   This is one of Moore's jokes ! What a rogue that clever little dog is !   Believe me very truly, dear sir,

Yours most sincerely,
W. L. BOWLES.[2]

Bowles to Murray

BREMHILL, April 15th, 1821.

My dear Sir
       My answer to Lord Byron will be printed by Thursday, and I hope publish'd by next Monday.

I understand the edition of Pope which has made

---

[1] It was Moore, Byron's friend, whose private commendation Bowles had repeated without mentioning his name.   When Byron heard the truth, he wrote Moore : " You see what comes of being familiar with parsons."

[2] Murray forwarded this and the following letters to Byron.   In consequence Byron on May 10th rescinded his order that his second *Letter to Murray* should be published.   He regarded it, in the light of Bowles's urbanity, as too severe.   " I am obliged to Mr. Bowles," he said, " and Mr. B. is obliged to me, for having restored him to good humour.   He is to write, and you to publish, what you please, *motto* and subject.   I desire nothing but fair play for all parties."   On June 22nd, when he had seen Bowles's formal reply, he added : " I can't go on disputing for ever,—particularly in a polite manner.   I suppose he will take being *silent* for *silenced*."

all this stir is out of print; at least more is charg'd for it at Bath in consequence of its scarcity. A new edition being at all events requir'd, I think it would be but fair to give me an opportunity merely of recording my conviction of those points in which I think myself to blame.

I would wish it to be said that I am satisfied myself I did wrong in alluding to " libertine love," and saying that his connection with Martha " might not have been pure and innocent." It might for what I know, certainly, and Lord Byron has put the circumstance in so strong [a light], and yet touched on it so kindly, that I would merely wish the new editor, in justice to the memory of Pope, to say that I am the first to acknowledge the injustice.

Some passages in the life I would leave out myself, relating to his duplicity, tho it is evident, in my opinion, thro all his letters, and I would gladly leave out the notes to the letters, which are not many, as it really looks as if I sought occasion to speak disrespectfully. There is nothing else in the life or the notes that I care about, but some allowance ought, in candour, to be granted to me, and if you will convey these sentiments to the editor I shall be oblig'd to you.[1]

As to Lord Byron, whether for or against the question on which we are not agreed, it is a most delightful publication, and I hope my answer will appear, not as a solemn discussion, but as a conversation,—with a scholar, and gentleman, and high poet,—upon an interesting poetical topic.[2]

There is nothing that can possibly give the slightest

---

[1] The new edition finally appeared, in 1824, under the editorship of William Roscoe. Roscoe attacked Bowles vigorously, and thus precipitated still further controversy.

[2] In June, 1821, William Hazlitt contributed anonymously to the *London Magazine* the best article of the entire controversy. He sneered at both Bowles and Byron.

umbrage, tho I am decided I have the advantage, not because he has not greater talents, but because he has not consider'd the question in all points of view.

Moore had the same opinion till I had a little conversation with him and promptly answer'd all he advanc'd. He then saw the point clearly. (For he was " the Midas," I tell you confidentially, who wrote, You have hit the nail on the head ! and I now tell you, more confidentially, it was Campbell who was hit in the head, not Pope.)[1]

To say truth, I have been more hurt than you can think about printing that little note. It was sent in a moment of kindness, and being in a great hurry, and not having time to request permission, I have been vex'd with myself ever since. I let the asterisks pass off as relating to Pope and not Campbell, fearing it might lead to misunderstanding, and I now tell you the secret, and should have burnt the pamphlet but for Gilchrist's intemperate personalities.

I hope what I have said will go no farther, but my chief purpose in writing is this, to request you will make my sentiments regarding Pope and Martha Blount known to the editor, and if I think this but fair, I should think it fairer still if, the subject being now of amicable and, I hope, pleasant discussion, you will be the publisher of my letter to Lord [Byron]. I am sure he would not be displeas'd, and the whole, I think, would look more in highest gentlemanly spirit between all, and then I would instantly bury every thing that might seem unkind in regard to all this business.

I care not a farthing about any profit. If any, it shall be yours, except what would pay the mere expense of printing.

If you should have no serious objection, have the goodness to write a line to me at Mr. Cruttwell's

---

[1] Bowles had substituted four asterisks for the name.

K

printing office, Bath, by return of post, and believe me, dear sir,

Very truly
Yours,
W. L. BOWLES.

Murray to Bowles

LONDON, *April* 15, 1821.

My dear Sir
I have had the pleasure of receiving your three very obliging letters, and most happy am I to find a controversy so purely critico-literary, likely to be conducted, on both sides, with such becoming amenity. You had received a copy of Lord Byron's Letter before I could send you one, as your first letter requested, but, at that time, the work was out of print.

I have not the least hesitation in accepting your proposal that I should be the publisher of your forthcoming answer to Lord Byron, and, if you will favour me with the title of it, I will announce it immediately.

I remain, dear sir,
Your obliged and faithful servant,
JOHN MURRAY.

Bowles to Murray

BREMHILL, *April* 17th, 1821.

My dear Sir
I am rejoic'd very much to think my pamphlet will enter the literary world under the same auspices as Lord Byron's. This is as it should be, and I am sure the conduct of the question will be such that you will not regret it. I shall feel it doubly incumbent on

me to preserve the tone of courtesy and amenity of which Lord Byron has set me such an example, and shall I say that I think the question itself both novel and interesting, now it is brought to a point of such argument.   I think I shall, under such auspicious sanction as you give me, print five hundred, unless I hear from you by to-morrow's post at Mr. Cruttwell's. The title for advertisement is—

A Letter to the Right Honorable Lord Byron on Poetical Criticism, in Answer to his Lordship's Letter on a Late Edition of Pope's Works, and on the Principles of Poetry
By the Revd. Wm. L. Bowles
He that Plays at Bowls (with the Sun and Moon?)
Must Expect Rubbers.—Old Proverb.

If you should [have] the slightest objection to this motto, let me know instantly.   But as Lord Byron's motto is the playful one:

I'll Play at Bowls.—Old Song,

I think neither he or you could possibly object to the old song being met by the old proverb.
                    I am, dear sir,
                            Your truly oblig'd friend, &c.,
                                W. L. Bowles.

Bowles to Murray

Sunday, [April 22 or 23, 1821].

Dear Sir
        The matter in answer to Lord Byron, for I have followed him in his delightful excursion[1] step by step, has led me a little farther than I expected.   I have therefore thought it best to divide the subject

---

[1] That is, in the search for images from nature and images from art.

into two letters. On Thursday evening at farthest four hundred copies of the letters will be sent by the mail-coach. Mr. Cruttwell thought it best to send the impression in quires (?), as you could get the pamphlet made up so much more expeditiously.

I hope you will not be sparing in getting it advertis'd, for which, if the sale should not cover it, I would cheerfully repay you, but of this I conceive there can be no doubt. If the whole impression shall be sold, I should be glad certainly to pay for the mere printing, but all beyond, of course, will be yours, as the liberty to print on your own account as many copies afterwards as you please.

I would wish you particularly to send a copy to the Bishop of London, Bishop of Hereford, Sir James Mackintosh, Sir Thomas Lawrence. My other friends, Lord Lansdowne, Sir George Beaumont, Lord Holland, Nares, &c., will doubtless have copies of you, and it is hardly worth sending them; but you will do as you like.

Our friend Crabbe is not generally consider'd as a sublime painter of any sublime imagery from Nature; but his description of the sea, I think, is as fine as ever was written. I have made much use of him, and hope both you and he will be pleas'd, but I should wish a copy to be sent to him from you, as what I have said will be more unexpected.

I should wish some of this part quoted in any literary journal, if you have influence with them.

I go the whole excursion with Lord Byron, and make my bow when we get from the coast of Africa (?) to Salisbury Plain. I really think you will be pleas'd if you can take the trouble of following us.

I trust Lord Byron will be pleas'd also. His philosophy of criticism is unsound, but his pictures are delightful, and I am sure, from the style, he does not care two pence about the philosophy.

I send you the corrected title, which I hope to see

in the Courier and Chronicle, &c.,—but this you
know best,—and that it will be announc'd.

I am, &c.,
Dear sir,
Very truly,
W. L. BOWLES.

On Monday, April 30th, will be publish'd Mr.
Bowles's Answer to Lord Byron. [The corrected
title follows.]

Bowles to Murray

Mr. Cruttwell's Printing Office, Bath,

April 24th, 1822.

Dear Sir

Being about to wind up all my critical accounts,
I am printing the third edition of Letters to Byron,
including part of the letter to Mr. Campbell, and a
small part of what was publish'd in answer to the
arguments of the Quarterly Review.

As Lord Byron published three editions of his letter
relating to me, I cannot for a moment suppose you
would, in justice, object to be the publisher of this
edition, as the two former had the advantage of your
name. The publication will be sent to London from
hence some time in the early part of May.

In this new version of part of my vindication in
answer to the Quarterly Review of 1820, I have put
out every passage that I thought might be personally
offensive to the writer in the Quarterly on Spence's
Anecdotes, tho that publication has been to me like
the opening of Pandora's box ! But it would be dis-
engenuous not to state that as the criticism in which
I was mention'd, contain'd some critical remarks
which were not call'd for by the subject, mainly by

way of being even (as in the case with Hobhouse[1]), I have also made a few critical remarks on some publish'd works, to shew from specimens what style in poetry ought to be avoided, as well as to lay down those principles by which I presume to appreciate the poetry of Pope and Milton. A very trifling but good-humour'd allusion to the last Quarterly will be made, with which I am sure the powerful writer of that article will not be displeas'd, and I remain, dear sir,

Very truly,
W. L. Bowles.

P.S.—I never saw or heard of Mr. Watts till I met him in London February last.

Bowles to Hurst and Robinson

Bremhill, Jan. 29, [1826].[2]

Mr. Bowles presents his compliments to Messrs. Hurst and Robinson, and writes to say that as they did not inclose the most important cancel, and that for which he was most entirely solicitous, he is afraid the post miscarried.

It was sent up by Tuesday's post, and he can only hope it was forgot to be sent with the cancell'd pages received to-day. He has to thank Messrs. Robinson

---

[1] Hobhouse was responsible for the passage against Bowles in the first edition of *English Bards and Scotch Reviewers*, and had otherwise offended Bowles. Some sarcastic references to Hobhouse in the reply to Byron almost drew the nobleman back into the controversy.

[2] The original of this letter is in the possession of Dr. Neilson. The letter indicates that Bowles was hopeful of setting his old persecutor, the *Edinburgh Review*, against the *Quarterly* for a renewal of the controversy now just ready to expire.

for their attention and trusts the first cancel has been completed and inserted, tho not sent—but if they have not received it at all, it will be of the most serious concern to him.

He begs an answer by return and again has to express his thanks for their ready and obliging manner of attending to his requests.

He would be glad to know whether any copies have been ordered. I rather think it may make some sensation at headquarters, as I intend it should, for such ignorance and falsehood with such effrontery were never united so much as in that Quarterly article.[1]

And I should be glad if Final Appeal and Ellen Gray inclos'd, could be conveyed at the same time ~~with the answer to the Quarterly~~ (*sic*) to the Editor of the Edinburgh. It is but fair to get friends, if possible, in all quarters when such nefarious a system has been pursued.

How many copies of Final Appeal remain? It should have been advertised, with the last.

Begging pardon for this detail

I am

Yours etc.

W. L. BOWLES.

---

[1] In 1825 Bowles replied to Roscoe's aspersions with his *Final Appeal to the Literary Public, Relative to Pope*. Roscoe rejoined the same year with a public letter to Bowles. In October, 1825, appeared in the *Quarterly* George Taylor's anonymous article *Pope's Works and Character*. Bowles in 1826 issued a pamphlet called *Lessons in Criticism to William Roscoe, Esq., . . . with Further Lessons in Criticism to a Quarterly Reviewer*. This pamphlet virtually ended the discussion; for neither Roscoe nor Taylor made further attack, and the *Edinburgh Review* remained aloof from the controversy.

Bowles to Rev. Dr. Bliss

No. 178 Piccadilly, London,
May 26, 1832.

Dear Sir[1]

Some days ago I wrote to my friend the President of Trinity, mentioning the name of Mr. D'Israeli, author of the commentaries on the reign of Charles 1st,[2] as a person, from literature, and independence, and fortune, and especially his laſt work, in every way worthy to receive the honorary academical diſtinction of L. L. D. I have heard nothing from Dr. Ingram on the subject, and almoſt suspect I may have made some miſtake as to my direction in town. I therefore write a few lines on the subject directly to you, requesting you will inform me, as far as from your conſtant intercourse with the members of convocation you might be enabled to judge, whether in these days of malignancy againſt church and ſtate, it would not be creditable to the university adorn'd by Clarendon and Sheldon, to offer some honorary diſtinction to the beſt hiſtorical defender of that king who died for our altars.[3] I have already spoken to Dr. Routh, who is entirely of my opinion, and should be glad to hear from you and Dr. Ingram, and remain

Very faithfully,
W. L. Bowles.

---

[1] Directed to Oxford. It is characteristic of Bowles that this impulsive application in behalf of a former adversary should be written at the very time he was bitterly enraged against Southey.

[2] *Commentaries on the Life and Reign of Charles I,* 5 volumes, 1828–30.

[3] On July 4, 1832, Oxford conferred the degree of D.C.L. upon Disraeli " as the biographer of Charles I."

Bowles to Mr. Miller

BREMHILL, *June 14th*, 1812.

Mr. Bowles presents his compliments to Mr. Miller[1] and informs him he has receiv'd Sir Richard Hoare's beautiful and splendid work very safe.

Having had the pleasure of seeing Mr. Miller in town, and knowing his great respectability as a publisher, Mr. Bowles is tempted to lay before him a project which he has had some time in view.

It is this. Mr. Bowles has finished a rather considerable poem, which for particular reasons he wishes to have publish'd without his name, and for the same reason not to have his usual publisher, that the author might not be even suspected.

In preference, therefore, to any one in London, Mr. Bowles applies to Mr. Miller, to know whether he would consent to become a publisher of a poem upon the terms following—

Only four hundred copies to be printed, without a name. The publisher to be at all the expense, and of course to be entitled to all the profit, if any, of the first impression.

Should the poem go off with sufficient success, then the publisher to have a power of printing as far as fifteen hundred, with Mr. Bowles' name, upon terms hereafter to be agreed on, but the author to retain the copy-right.

---

[1] A London publisher, whose business Murray bought in 1812.

If Mr. Miller has his hands full, or is averse to publish for Mr. Bowles on these terms, Mr. Bowles implicitly trusts that what he has said may be an entire secret.

Mr. Bowles thinks it right for Mr. Miller's information to state that the poem consists of six books of about 250 lines each book, [and] would make a handsome small octavo volume. [It] is a story founded on historical fact, and related to the great political circumstances of the Spaniards in America, which in some degree gives it a present interest as connected with the existing war in Spain.[1]

.   .   .   .   .   .

If Mr. Miller should think an impression of four hundred too few for any chance of profit, Mr. Bowles would not object to the impression being five hundred, but not more, for the sake of another edition with the author's name and preface.

Mr. Bowles would have no objection to read the first book to Mr. Miller, but he wishes at present the subject to be a secret, as well as the name.

The poem was written at the express solicitation of Mr. Rogers, Mr. Bowles having never attempted a poem of the kind, and Mr. Rogers flattering him that he should succeed. Mr. Rogers (of St. James' Place) is therefore the only living person to whom the circumstance is known.

---

[1] The poem was published anonymously as *The Missionary* in 1813. In 1815 and 1816 the revised second and third editions appeared, with Bowles's name. In the story, Lautaro, an Indian who has been torn from his home in boyhood by the Spaniards, accompanies an expedition under Valdivia against his own people. At the crisis of the battle he turns against the Spaniards and causes their defeat. In a subordinate part of the story a humane missionary who also accompanies the force secures Lautaro's forgiveness for Zarinel, a wandering minstrel who has won the heart of Lautaro's sister Olola and then has left her.

Murray to Bowles

LONDON, *June 24th*, 1812,
Wednesday

Sir

Mr. Miller, in consequence of your permission, has done me the favor of communicating to me your letter upon the subject of a confidential publication of a new poem. This I shall have much pleasure in undertaking upon the following conditions, which will, I trust, meet your approbation.

That the First Edition consisting of five hundred copies shall be printed at Mr. Murray's sole expense and risque and that Mr. Murray shall be entitled to the whole profit, if any, upon this First Edition—this Edition to be published without the author's name.

Should the First Edition go off with sufficient success, then Mr. Murray shall have the power of printing any number not exceeding fifteen hundred (unless a greater impression may be hereafter mutually agreed upon) at the sole cost and risque of Mr. Murray, and that of such edition the author shall be entitled to one half of such profit, if any, as shall arise after the sale of the impression. The copyrights to remain the property of the author, whose name shall appear in this Second Edition.

I have extended the first impression to five hundred copies, as no smaller number would do more than pay the expenses. The condition respecting the second impression involves a remuneration which will not be thought too great for the risque upon both.

Mr. Miller communicated to me the anxieties expressed in your second letter, to which I can only offer the insurance of the most honourable secrecy. It may be time to begin the printing in December or

January and to bring out the poem in February or March when the town is full.

I beg the favour of your opinion upon the terms I have taken the liberty of proposing and I remain,

Sir,

Your obedient servant,

JOHN MURRAY.

Bowles to Murray

BREMHILL, *June* 26*th*, 1812.

Mr. Bowles will have no objection to the terms Mr. Murray has propos'd respecting the publication of a poem, and Mr. Bowles will wait upon Mr. Murray or send the copy some time between this and November next. Mr. Bowles relies on Mr. Murray's honorable secrecy, and of the anonymous publication only asks about a dozen copies for himself.

Mr. Bowles suggests to Mr. Murray whether it would not be adviseable to wait for the publication of Mr. Scott's and Mr. Southey's next poems. It would not answer (?) for a poem of six books to come out nearly at the same time with theirs. This, however, is left for Mr. Murray's determination.

Bowles to Murray

BREMHILL, *Decbr.* 20*th*, 1812.

Mr. Bowles presents his compliments to Mr. Murray. The title of the poem is

Lautaro, or
The Avenger of his Country.

Mr. Bowles confidently trusts that he may rely upon Mr. Murray's concealment of the author's name, which is not known to his most intimate friends. One person only, who suggested the circumstance, knows any thing of the intention. This is Mr. Rogers, of St. James's Place.

Mr. B. more particularly wishes the publication by himself should be kept a secret from any persons connected with the writers of the Quarterly Review.

There is only one copy of the other books, and if they should be lost in the carriage, they could not be replac'd: it would be best therefore, for fear of accident, that Mr. Murray should have them when Mr. Bowles comes to town, probably the latter end of Jany., if that would be time enough for this season.

Murray to Bowles

ALBEMARLE STREET,
Tuesday,
[*Between Dec.* 20 *and* 24, 1812].

Dear Sir

I beg leave to assure you of my resolution to preserve, most faithfully, your secret.

It is very desirable in announcing a work, particularly a poem, *without* an author's name, to be a little explanatory of the subject, because it must be, at first, by that alone that strangers may be tempted to send for it, and therefore I would be glad to receive by return of post, such particulars of the subject, (which you think it prudent to communicate,) as may be likely to interest the public—that is to say, if you feel with me the propriety and advantage of a more detailed announcement. With your *name* to it any thing would be sufficiently attractive, but without a name some attraction must be created.

I am, sir,
Your faithful servant,
JOHN MURRAY.

Do I read rightly Lautaro ?

Bowles to Rogers

BREMHILL, *Feb.* 18*th*, 1813.

Dear Rogers

As your great ship the Columbus[1] is on the deep, . . I must expect a little of your kind assistance toward the launching my shallop. I was pleas'd with your observation that it was necessary in a poem of such a subject as mine to throw into the region of South America as much interest as possible from Europe. This indeed has been the case, as you will find when you read the whole. It begins and ends with Europe, and the story of the missionary more immediately connects the poem with interests on this side of the Atlantic. Still, however, I was not impress'd with the idea of the absolute essentiality of this pervading light, till I heard your very just remark, which, you see, even in the noise of Piccadilly was not lost upon me.

The ballad of the Cid, of which I was in some doubt, which forms the sixth book, is therefore peremptorily retained, and I was thinking, as a Spanish minstrel is introduc'd, tho without reference to the story, that it would break the uniformity of the first book if he were thrown into a little song when the Spanish camp is describ'd at night by moonlight. [Bowles here quotes the proposed song.]

Here will be a more immediate contrast between the feelings of Lautaro, in his own country, and the wandring minstrel who has none.

If you approve, get the lines inserted in the place. It will come in the second sheet, so there is full time, and pray hurry Murray. If you borrow the first book of the poem from Murray, which is copied out very

---

[1] Rogers published his fragmentary epic *Columbus* in 1810, but he had printed it privately two years before.

fair, you can insert the passage in five minutes, before it comes to the compositor's hands. I told Murray if he thought it advisable, on his own account, I should not object to his telling Gifford the name of the author, knowing the acumen as well as liberality of his own criticisms, and relying on his secrecy.

Yours ever,

W. L. BOWLES.

Bowles to Murray

BREMHILL, *April 4th*, 1813.

Dear Sir

When I requested you to shew a sheet, after it was printed, to Mr. Rogers or Lord Byron, it was under the idea that it would not possibly make a delay of more than one day's post. It certainly would not be adviseable if it must prevent the poem being publish'd at the only season when it seems to me there is a fair opening.

I am now going from home for a week, so that I cannot have a sheet before next Saturday, but if one should be ready on Tuesday next I shall get it on Wednesday if you will direct it to me at John Benett's, Esq., Pyt-house, near Shaftesbury, Dorset.

If you have spoken to Lord Byron, I think you had better tell him that I feel a confidence in him. I wish we could persuade [him] to write about twenty lines as an introduction to the sixth book,[1] allusive to present circumstances, the battle of Salamanca, and the annihilation of the French invading army in Russia. Besides, he owes, as he will acknowledge, some amends to me for quoting[2] me as the author of some nonsense which, he now knows, I never wrote,

[1] The passage was not written.
[2] In *English Bards and Scotch Reviewers*.

at least with the interpretation put to it. We had an explanation on this subject, and he acknowledg'd how wrong he had been very ingenuously. This is entre nous.

I am, &c.,

Yours very sincerely,

W. L. BOWLES.

I have written an introduction myself which I left at Salisbury. . . . It will be some time before you come to the sixth book and before that time I shall be in town, when I mean to bring them, together with the entire sixth book which you have not got. If however we could get Lord Byron to write a few lines, I need not say I should acknowledge it in the handsomest manner I could.

Murray to Bowles

LONDON, *Aug.* 29, 1814,
Monday

Dear Sir

I am truly happy in having had the pleasure of hearing from you, for I much desired to communicate though in these days of universal migration I was uncertain how to address you.

I have not, of course, printed any more copies of your poem and the advertisement which you observed was intended at once to shew that the first edition was out of print and to announce the new edition which is really much called for and which we should now begin to print. I should propose to you to print 750 copies of this second edition in foolscap octavo, the same size as Mr. Rogers' Poems, which is indeed the most popular if not the most appropriate.

Make as much improvement as you can but do not add without retrenching also and you will ensure success. If the poem had all its beauties condensed into two thirds of its present size, I do think I could sell thousands, and it is a great pleasure to be universally read. I entreat you to pardon the obtrusive sincerity of this remark, to the truth of which I pledge myself. When you are quite ready for press send me up a good portion to begin with and indeed I will thank you to give me notice for I purpose going to the Continent on Tuesday week, and to Scotland afterwards, and if you are so disposed I could set the printing a-going before I leave London. Do not fail if you send any MSS. to begin with to tell me as nearly as you can how many lines the whole will consist of, as this must determine the size of the page, &c., and do me the favor to add the probable *additional* quantity of Notes.—Humboldt's personal Narrative of his Travels are just published here, at least the two first volumes, which you ought to have.

Will you if you see your odd (old ?) friend Mr. Lucas remind him of Wolfe's Letters, which I am still desirous to see ?

I trust that you continue well and with best compliments remain,

Dear sir,
Your faithful servant,
JOHN MURRAY.

I have just seen the advertisement of a *certain* poem which I shall send for.

Bowles to Murray

My dear Sir   BREMHILL, *Decber*. 6*th*, 1814.

I should have written to you before but as you talk'd of going to the continent, when I heard from you last, I thought probable you were not yet return'd.

L

The edition may be set about instantly, if you have a copy, as there will be no particular alterations in the first sheet. I should wish to see you myself, but if I cannot come to London at this time, you may depend upon receiving my interleav'd copy from which to print on Tuesday or Wednesday the 13th by the Revd. Mr. Money, who is going to town. I have added an episodical story, which I hope will relieve the main narrative, and also obviate the most material objection I have had to the conduct of the poem, that the Indian girl who is particularly describ'd in the first book was not made enough of in the subsequent part of the poem. I have endeavour'd to cut down the rest, but fear I cannot bring it to your standard of compression. Another person perhaps might do it better, and I should have no objection to leave out every thing not absolutely essential to the narrative, (bating the machinery) if I could get any one to mark every unnecessary ornament with a severe eye.

In consequence, I verily believe, of my name being known, I have seen an illiberal notice taken both of me and the poem in a satirical (?) publication.[1] Inform me, if you know or have heard, the name of the writer, as I think I ought to take some notice of it in the preface to this edition.

I could wish that not more than five hundred copies should be printed if this will answer your purpose.

A friend of mine (a gentleman of very large fortune in this county), Mr. Benett of Pyt-House, has in his possession a whole trunk full of original letters,

---

[1] Perhaps *The Modern Dunciad, a Satire*, (1814). It was anonymous, but George Daniel was the author. It is outspoken against Bowles :

" While Bowles exists, can satire want a dunce ? "

on account of his own poetry and his edition of Pope. It mentions *The Missionary* as his.

written in the beginning of the civil wars by those who were the great actors on the king's side. There are not less than 63 letters in Charles's own hand writing, to Rupert, from the year 1642 to '45. Letters also in their own hand writing from Secretary Nicholas (fifty or sixty), Lord Digby, Northampton, Sir Jacob Ashby, &c., and almost all the distinguish'd persons. Among these are five or six and twenty from the ancestor of Lord Byron. As Mr. Benett talks of publishing them, the collection may be worth your notice, but I only throw out this hint.

If Lord Byron should have any curiosity to see the particular letters I mention'd of his ancestor, I could shew them to him when I come to London, if you think it worth while to mention the circumstance to his Lordship.

I am, dear sir,
With great truth,
Yours very sincerely,
W. L. BOWLES.

Have you seen an account of my residence here in the Gentleman's Magazine for September?[1] If not, procure it, and I need not say how happy I should be at any time to shew you that parsonage and this part of the county of Wilts.

Murray to Bowles

ALBEMARLE ST., *Saturday*
[*Between Dec. 6 and* 13, 1814].

Dear Sir

As the 13th is now near I prefer waiting until then when you are so good as to say that you will

---

[1] The author was Archdeacon Nares.

spare your corrected copy of the poem, of which although I might collect a few sheets, yet I certainly have no compleat copy.

I am happy to hear of your addition which from your description will both relieve and increase the interest of the narrative.

You are not aware perhaps that 500 copies will not yield any reasonable profit, and may require a price somewhat higher, as the price of each individual copy must be more. I would have recommended 750. But I beg you to regulate that point entirely by your own feelings. I shall be perfectly satisfied by the certainty of its sale and by the reputation which always attaches to the publisher of an original and interesting work.

I entreat you not to heed the contemptible article upon your book to which you allude and of which I know nothing but your notice of it. You have the most gratifying praise in the judicious and flattering criticisms which were made upon the work before the author was known and you should not allow the spite of some low fellow—I make no doubt the author is— to diminish one jot of the satisfaction to which you are so honourably entitled.

I feel very much interested in your account of the curious collection of letters which have been discovered at your friend Mr. Benett's and I should feel myself most particularly obliged if you used your influence to procure for me the publication of a work of such high interest and respectability. If you require the additional influence of the Marquis of Lansdowne, who has called upon me more than once in company with Mr. Benett, I could perhaps get a letter from Dugald Stewart (who is a relation of Mrs. Murray) to him, but I think even in this quarter the exertion of your kindness would prove satisfactory.

I read your account of these letters to Lord Byron and he desired me with his compliments to assure you that he would feel highly gratified by a sight of those of his ancestor.

. . . .

Scott's poem may be expected in a fortnight. Roderick is a very fine poem.

Vale,

Jno. Murray.

Southey to Bowles

Keswick, 21 Feby., 1815.

My dear Sir[1]

Murray kept your secret well, when I expressed to him my admiration of the Missionary, and asked to whom I was indebted for what had given me so much pleasure. I could be angry with myself for not having discovered you,—but it never occurred to me that a name should be suppreſt which would have carried with it so sure a recommendation to so wide a circle of readers;—and I thought also that you had been well versed in Spanish, which the author of the Missionary seemed not to be, by the manner in which *Campeador* is accented:—It should be Campĕădŏr.

The alteration of which you do me the honour to ask my opinion, will certainly add much to the intereſt of the poem. I admire your conception of Valdivia's charaſter,—and I love your missionary: tho the prieſt who in reality shared Valdivia's fate moſt probably heartily deserved it. The clergy who accompanied the firſt conquerors were as bad as the conquerors themselves. . . .

I thought you were versed in Spanish literature, because the solemn and impressive opening of your ode upon the Battle of the Nile[2] very much resembles

---

[1] Directed to Bath.　　[2] Published in 1799.

that of one of the finest poems in the Spanish language,
—Herrera's Ode upon the Battle of Lepanto.

Whenever I may be travelling westward (or rather
southward) it will give me great pleasure to halt
awhile with you:—but my ties with that part of
England are much loosened. Death has cut up the
dearest of them by the roots, and my heart fails me
when I look that way.—According to the ordinary
course of things I ought to have been settled at this
time in the west of England upon a fair fortune, but
it has been my lot to be twice disinherited by near
relations to whom I never gave cause or shadow of
offence. They were both cases of that kind of in-
sanity which is not cognizable by law. Here in this
beautiful country I am too far from libraries, and too
far from my friends: and going but seldom to London,
I am old enough whenever I leave them to feel very
strongly the uncertainty of seeing them again. These
things make me sometimes think of moving, and Bath
generally presents itself as the place where a man of
limited means may enjoy most comforts.

And now, my dear sir, farewell. I am indebted to
you for many hours of deep enjoyment, and for great
improvement in our common art,—for your poems
came into my hands when I was nineteen[1] and I *fed*
upon them. Our booby critics talk of *schools*, and if
they had had common discernment they might have
perceived that I was of your school. But they are as
deficient in judgement as they are in candour and in
common honesty.

Believe me
Very truly and respectfully yours,
ROBERT SOUTHEY.

---

[1] Southey was born Aug. 12, 1774.

Bowles to Murray

READING, *May 30th*, 1815.

My dear Sir

I shall be in town Friday or Saturday morning, when I hope to see you. The poem is finish'd all but the title-page, &c., which I shall bring with me or send to-morrow; but I would not have it printed off till I had consulted you about one or two points as to what I have said in the preface and dedication.

As only five hundred copies are printed, I shall not think of taking any share myself should there be a profit on the sale, but would request four and twenty copies for some of my private friends who probably would not purchase.

I remain, &c.,

Yours most truly,

W. L. BOWLES.

I am finishing some sermons to plain people, with a preface giving a statement of the occasion. They will be entitled, " Sermons on the Doctrines and Dispositions of Christians. . . ."[1] These are now printing in Bath, but I hope you will allow me the honour of your name as London publisher. I would also hope you would not object to be book-seller and publisher to a kind of historical work, of the same small size, on the aberrations from the plain sense of the Bible in all ages.

Southey to Bowles

KESWICK, *5th Jany.*, 1816.

My dear Sir

You ask me a difficult question when you desire me to say what are the faults of your poem.

[1] Published by Murray in 1815.

Well as I was acquainted with it I read it once more to see if the reperusal would enable me to discover them, and in truth I do not see how you can improve it by any alteration. I could have wished your Indian maid had been spared,—because I am arrived at that age when men like to be spared from as many painful feelings as possible;—in our youth we love to shed tears over fictitious sorrows,—as we grow older we have none to spare for them, and find too much cause for melancholy thoughts ever to have them willingly excited. But you could not have disposed of her otherwise and when happiness has been rendered impossible, death becomes the desirable termination.

In the way of petty criticism I can find very little to say. . . .

I do not like to have a narrative interrupted by episodes; and therefore I would rather see the Ballad of the Cid transplanted to your miscellaneous poems,[1] and a shorter song introduced upon the conquest of Chili, which would give more force to the five (fine ?) lines that immediately follow. You have here all that I can invent in the way of fault-finding. Two causes have hitherto prevented me from saying what I propose to offer in its praise,—first, that I have been three months from home, during which time I went thro great part the new kingdom of the Netherlands; and secondly, that ever since my return I have been busy in putting into six-lined stanzas the Poet's Pilgrimage to the Feet (?) of the Belle Alliance,[2] with what success a short time will determine, as I hope soon to complete my task.

I could not feel otherwise than gratified and obliged by the latter part of your letter. My habits, feelings and inclinations would long since have induced me to enter the church if the terms of admission

---

[1] This Bowles did, substituting Southey's for Rogers's advice. In the first edition the " Song of the Cid " had ended Canto VI.

[2] This appeared as *The Poet's Pilgrimage to Waterloo* in 1816.

had not presented an insuperable bar. It is not that I could subscribe to any other articles in preference; —there are points which I desire, as far as concerns myself individually, to leave indefinite. Meantime the Establishment cannot have a more zealous and conscientious advocate, a more willing conformist, or a more sincere and grateful follower.

I shall read your discourses with much interest;— Murray is frequently sending parcels to me, and they may come thro that channel. I hope Sir George Beaumont will succeed in tempting you to visit this beautiful country, where you may even find hints for Chilese landscape.[1] The grandest sights which I have ever beheld, or can ever hope to behold, have been from the summit of Skiddaw,—which I have within an easy morning's walk.

Believe me, my dear sir,
Yrs. most truly and with sincere respect,
ROBERT SOUTHEY.

---

[1] Among Bowles's papers is a scrap-book containing, in his hand, a list of places through which he would pass " to the lakes." The list includes Coniston Water, Hawkeshead, Bowness across Windermere, Ambleside, Rydal, and Keswick. The scrap-book is dated 1807. But there is no sure evidence that Bowles ever visited that region.

MISCELLANEOUS

Linley to Bowles

COWLEY PLACE, *July* 23*d*, 1797.

My dear Sir,

I keep in mind with much satisfaction the arrangement we made during our short interview at Glocester, but as certain circumstances have occurred since which will prevent my fulfilling my promise so early as I could wish, I write that you may not suppose I am forgetful thereof, or so stupidly inattentive to the pleasure and profit I must experience in your society.

Cowley Place is the seat of Mr. Jackson, Junr., a son of the celebrated composer, and an Indian crony of mine.[1] I did not originally intend to stay here longer than a fortnight, but there are certain attractions in real hospitality when seconded by the charms of a fine country and still finer women, which I am weak enough to find irresistible. I fancy you know something of the family of the Barings at Exmouth. Mr. Jackson married one of the sisters, and here are three unmarried under the very roof with me, all sensible, young, and beautiful—full of conversation, full of poetry, and music ! How the plague then could I remain invulnerable to any solicitation that promised a longer enjoyment of such society? I could not. I was born under the same planet with you, my friend, and tho' you move in so much more exalted a sphere, and enjoy its brightest influence, yet as I have now and

[1] Linley was in India, in the service of the East India Company, from 1790 to 1796.

then caught a glimpse thro' the gloom, I may be said
to have engendered some small particles of its splen-
dour. I have consented to prolong my visit to the
fourteenth of August, and shall the day after bend
my course to Donhead by the conveyance you pointed
out to me at Glocester. If this time does not suit
you, let me know and I will make the requisite alterations according to the time you shall point out.[1] But
give me a line at all events acknowledging the receipt
of this, and direct to the care of W. Jackson, Jun.,
Esqr., Cowley Place, near Exon.

A worthy baronet in this neighbourhood claims
acquaintance with you, vizt. : [tear] Stafford Northcote.
He has a very charming estate contiguous to Cowley.

Your poems are the order of the day here. In truth
I know not where they are not so. One of the Miss
Barings—and I think the prettiest—was reading the
sonnet to Hope this morning, and I happened to say
I was going to pay a visit to the author soon. ' Bless
me ! ' (Half a dozen at a time). ' Do you know
Mr. Bowles ? I should like to be acquainted with
him, of all things ! ' Happy dog, groaned I.—I am
afraid of disgracing you, Bowles, but I should like to
set some of your words to music. I tried once, but
could not then please myself. Adieu !

Sincerely yours,
WILLIAM LINLEY.

Linley to Mrs. Bowles

FURNIVALS INN CHAMBS.,

Dear Mrs. Bowles,   *Augt. 3d,* [1832].
    If I were to leave unanswered the heavy
charge you have brought against me of being guilty

---

[1] The visit was deferred till September, when Coleridge also was
a guest at Donhead.

of " excesses which are distressing to every one, and lamentable to see," I should appear to plead guilty to it.

Indeed, my excellent friend, convinced as I am of your most sincere regard, and that you would not mean to wound my feelings, I must nevertheless own that I am very much hurt by your very strong expressions, and cannot help fearing that some exaggerated story has been told you of me, which you have not done me justice if you have believed.[1]

That I may occasionally have drank wine to a certain point of elevation, even at Bremhill, I will not deny; but if I have been so besotted as to have justly deserved the character your words would imply, a character " quite altered " as you say from my proper one, it were better that I kept away from the risk of giving further offence, and withdrew from society altogether.

I am naturally of a social turn, and like my glass of wine;—I will not deny it;—but there are some dosey, formal people—and Wiltshire is one, who if a laugh happens to be too incorrectly loud, or an argument too ardently pursued in conversation, immediately attributes the temporary excitement to drunkenness,— and if *I* am to be so tried and so judged, I would, on no consideration, expose myself to such misrepresentations of conduct. You surely cannot seriously fear that I shall run riot at Bremhill, and disturb the serenity of the friends you are expecting ?—If so, anxious as I am to preserve the small remains of regard that you and Mr. Bowles may still retain for me, I had better, perhaps, postpone my visit.

But I won't think so. You have had stories told of me that are not true, or else that have been greatly exaggerated. I have, since last autumn, been very

---

[1] This letter seems, happily, to have put an end to the misunderstanding. Upon Linley's death Bowles wrote in the *Gentleman's Magazine* (June, 1835) an eulogistic sketch of his friend.

much annoyed by dizziness—a nervous affection only, but still of a nature to have rendered the excesses you mention probably fatal to me, had I indulged in them.

The rest of your letter, my dear friend, is delightfully satisfactory, except when you mention the death of my old acquaintance Goffer (?) We quite agree in politics. The Whigs are destroying us, and I think you must regret that Lord Lansdowne is one of the batch. Moore I have not seen for ages. *He* is a downright Radical, I doubt—but Whigs and Radicals are now the same.

God bless you, my dear Mrs. B. ! And believe me that I shall be able to defend myself better than you are aware of from the attacks that " some good-natured friends " may have made upon me. And so I remain

Ever most faithfully yrs.,

W. Linley.

Bowles to Murray

Bremhill, *June 9th*, 1829.

Dear Sir

Amid your more splendid announcements, I must call your attention to a *poor* poet.

My second edition of " Days Departed," much enlarg'd, with the addition of a tale by way of episode, in a smaller volume to suit my other poems, is now printed. But have you got, or have you forgotten, my picture ? Is it engraved ?

The volume, done up, will be sent to you (240 copies) on account of the plates which you can get inserted, or would it be best to send the impression in sheets ? If the plate is not finish'd, or perhaps forgotten, the poem must be publish'd without it.

I have received a letter from Galignani of Paris, to say he is going to print the whole of my poems, but

I should wish only those selected which I think would be most popular.

If you are busy, let your son or any one write a line instanter. Will you present a copy to Mr. Lockhart? He is perhaps sick of the sight of poems of this appearance, but I have some lines[1] on Sir Walter Scott, and I should hope if he begins he would read my poem to the end.

.   .   .   .

Let me hear, and believe me, &c.,

Very truly,

W. L. BOWLES.

Pickering to Moore

LONDON, *Nov.* 9, 1835.

My dear Sir

I must first thank you for your kind letter and trust that the following will at least prove that I am no party to the abuse of the Revd. Mr. Bowles. As a publisher I cannot at all times chuse and refuse the works that are offered to me, as from old connexions or the publishing of other works of writers I do not think that I can fairly refuse to publish, provided the works are not libelous. In the present instance the Modern Dunciad is a *sixth* edition[2] but the others were not published by me and the book, I think, must have been out nearly 15 years with the same passages which are now objected to. It is not however my taste to publish such works as the Modern Dunciad, but having taken it, I cannot with propriety retract.

The fact of the review by Mr. Mitford of the book in the Gentleman's Magazine,[3] of which I am a pro-

---

[1] A sonnet.   [2] Published 1835.

[3] November, 1835. John Mitford (1781–1859) was a miscellaneous writer and a loyal admirer of Bowles.

prietor, shews that I am equally open to publish in defense of Mr. Bowles and to admit a personal attack upon the author of the Modern Dunciad, which has also brought me into disgrace by the author and his friends, so that I who was really ignorant of the contents of both articles until published am the greatest sufferer. The author of the Dunciad is not a little sore from the review in Blackwood of September and the present one in the Gentleman's, which he considers much worse.

From what I know of the writings of Mr. Bowles I should, had I known of the critique, have hesitated to have been the publisher, because I now have before me a very different encomium in the Life of Izaak Walton[1] which is now printing and to which I can most cordially assent.

I am not aware that I can now do more than to express my regret that I should have been instrumental in publishing anything that should give him pain or displeasure. Still should Mr. B. consider that the attack ought not to be passed over, I beg that he will not consider me individually, as the author is in circumstances to defend himself or to pay for his misdeeds. In conclusion I beg again to thank you for your kind interference and if necessary I may perhaps hereafter again trouble you.

I remain, my dear sir,
Your obliged servant,
W. PICKERING.

---

[1] This was attached to a two-volume edition of *The Complete Angler* (1836). The editor, Sir Harry Nicholas, makes complimentary references to Bowles.

Bowles to J. Mitford

BREMHILL, *April 8th,* 1836.

My dear Sir[1]
  I am juſt returned to this quiet angulus " mihi me reddentis agelli " and here I have juſt received, directed to Salisbury, Mr. Pickering's and your kind letter.

He can pick up *Patmos*[2] somewhere if not at Bulcock's—16 Hamilton place, new Road.

He may begin the Sonnets as there printed—all of which are correct and many as they were *firſt* meditated—and after the sonnet on the " Cherwell," Oxford include that on a Lady,

" When laſt we parted," &c.

This finishes the first series of sonnets—written in early youth from disappointed passion. The tale is *too* affecting to me, even at these years, to enter on— if I pursue my " Scenes and Shadows of Remembrance ! "

Pickering can begin printing directly, as when I come to London the 3d of May I can look over as far as he may have got, according to my scheme in laſt letter.

I do not care two-pence about being indemnified for expense, but if Mr. Pickering thinks it beſt to print 500 he may do so. My chief object was to leave on record what I had written in this way, taking the beſt of the Poetical compositions, with the arrangement beginning as I have marked in my laſt letter.

  [1] The letter is addressed in Pickering's care, Chancery Lane, London.
  [2] *St. John in Patmos,* the later editions of which had contained selections from Bowles's minor poems. Bowles and Pickering were now beginning to consider a collected edition of Bowles's works, but the plan was not carried through.

I thought it best to have an octavo size as it would suit the size of my " Scenes and Shadows,"[1] for which I purpose having engravings should I go on.

Apropos of this projected publication, the moment Murray of Albemarle Street read this brochure of mine, he wrote to say that " upon his word " he thought it " so attractive (this was his expression) that he should be happy to publish it in weekly numbers," pay all costs of printing and engravings, take upon himself " every expense and give me half the profits."

This was the most magnificent, and I might say the only, offer of the kind I have had in my Life, or Poetical Life !

I wrote to say that I thought the offer was " princely," but that no pecuniary advantage could tempt me to engage in a weekly job ! It might be otherwise, perhaps, if the work were to be monthly instead of weekly, but as to profit it never had any consideration with me, notwithstanding what " Daniel says " or sings.

Since this, I have heard nothing from " John " of Albemarle Street. But if he chooses to publish, I have made him the first offer and I shall be glad, if he only is willing, to do so at my expense, and not his own.

Finally, Mr. Pickering must get or borrow my last edition, or rather (illegible from seal) of *Patmos* from the volume containing it, begin—(illegible) with the sonnets in the one after (illegible), but nota bene——

The sonnet on Bamborough Castle must be the 2d after " Landing at Tynemouth." The order after this is right in all the editions, and the note on Bamborough in the first edition should be retain'd on account of what is said of Crew and my Grandfather in Scenes and Shadows.

[1] A brochure bearing this title (1835) was the basis of *Scenes and Shadows of Days Departed*, which Pickering published in 1837.

I am afraid I have put you to a somewhat perplexing job, but on considering it, I hope there will be no difficulty to you or Mr. Pickering, and believe [me]
Your oblig'd friend and ser't
W. L. Bowles.

Note my " Monument to Chillingworth and Hooker " in Urbanus's next magazine.[1]

1 volume is mark'd already.   After " Hope, an Allegorical Sketch," omitting preface, to be call'd
" A Vision of Hope," two other of the same kind from IVth volume to follow to be call'd
2 " A Vision of Time "
3 " A Vision of the Winds "
A Vision of Poetry—
When I come we can arrange whole.

P.S.   If Murray declines publishing Scenes and Shadows, it would be best to include them just as they are in the Introduction to this edition or [as] a few more chapters, making three volumes—one of Introduction and two of poems.   I am sure I have chalk'd out as much as Pickering can do till I come.

P.S.   I cannot close this letter without again thanking you, but were you aware that some verbal inaccuracies appear in your admirable criticism ?
" *Stay* motionless " is " Hang motionless "
" Promontories shrine "—shine.
" Stretchy "—stretching.   Excuse these remarks on mere errors of the printer, I suppose.
Brave dog—lean dog
Head—Heed

---

[1] Three generations of the Nichols family were successively editors of the *Gentleman's Magazine*.   The editorial pseudonym of each was Sylvanus Urban.

Pickering to Bowles

LOND., *Nov.* 16, 1837.

My dear Sir
 The *total* (?) of printing your little volume[1] including portrait and boarding up 71 copies which you have either had or have been presented to your friends is £74/1/10. Now if agreeable to you to send me £50, I shall be quite satisfied.
 Mr. Mitford says you have given [him] the copyrights of your poems and which I think I understand him that he will give to me as he cannot make any use of it. Should you, as you once named, leave me the copyright of your poems, I shall have much pleasure at a future day printing the *entire* collection. I like *opera omnia's* better than parts, and I should think that they would pay their expenses, if not too many corrections. This however I leave entirely to yourself, to do as you may now or hereafter think right. Should they come to me at any time, I think no one will feel more interested for the author.
 Many of my friends are much pleased with the little volume. If I could have foreseen how slender it would have been, I should have used *thicker* paper.
 I remain, my dear sir,
 Ever most truly yrs.,
 W. PICKERING.

Pickering to Bowles

LOND., *May* 8, 1838.

My dear Sir
 I am glad to find that you are at Bremhill and in good spirits. Your little volume has gone off very well. I have 163 left and shall be ready to go to press

---

[1] *Scenes and Shadows of Days Departed.*

whenever the copy is prepared for a thicker one, or two if you please.

I hope you are aware that when I first charged 7/6 for the book, it was under the supposition that *it was to bear all the charges*, but that I afterwards made it 5/—, as it was too high.

Mr. Mitford I expect in town daily who will, I am sure, do every thing to please you—and as for making the book I will do my best. I should much like to see Bremhill again, but at present I have so much to keep me at home that I dare not think of it.

. . . .

With kind remembrance to Mrs. Bowles,
I remain, my dear sir,
Yr. faithful and obliged Sevt.,
W. PICKERING.

Sydney Smith to Bowles

COMBE FLOREY,
TAUNTON,
December 6, 1838.

My dear Sir

Depend upon it I will crucify Simon and make him as detestable to good churchmen (?) as is Simon Magus. I shall immediately procure, read, and profit by your pamphlet.[1] Bishops should not write at all, seldom speak, and confine themselves to voting.

Ever truly yours,
SYDNEY SMITH.

[1] In 1836 Bowles wrote three indignant pamphlets, and in 1838 one, against a proposal by the church commissioners to transfer to the bishops the patronage of deans and chapters. The pamphlet of 1838 was in answer to the Bishop of Bristol and Gloucester.

FOUR ANONYMOUS REVIEWS BY
COLERIDGE

I

INTRODUCTORY NOTE

" ARE you not connected with the *Critical Review ?* "
Lamb inquired of Coleridge in a letter written July 5,
1796.   An answer to the question may be found in
Coleridge's letter to Poole on December 12th of the
same year: " I receive about forty guineas yearly from
the ' Critical Review ' and the new ' Monthly Magazine.' "   Not only has the connection with the
periodical been known, but from hints that were
dropped at the time, for example in Lamb's letters
of June 10 and December 2, 1796, it might be possible
to learn, or at least to surmise, what were some of the
contributions of which Coleridge was author.

In the case of the four reviews here reproduced,
however, there is none of the uncertainty which
attaches to conjecture, well buttressed though it be.
In the letter written to Bowles about March, 1797,
Coleridge states unequivocally that he has been
reviewing for the *Critical Review*, along with other
romances, *The Monk*, *The Italian*, and *Hubert de
Sevrac*.   He leaves us, therefore, no more difficult a
task than searching through the columns of the
periodical for the articles in question.   The one on
The Monk had just been published; the other two did
not appear until the following year.   We learn from
the discussion of *The Italian* that Coleridge had
treated *The Mysteries of Udolpho* as well, though at a

period so much earlier that he may not then have been a regular " hireling " of the *Critical Review*.

The only consideration which can disturb us for a moment is the possibility that Coleridge, when he spoke of *The Italian*, may have meant James Boaden's dramatization of it (*The Italian Monk*), which was noticed in the *Critical Review* for November, 1797. But the internal evidence which the review of the drama affords unites with the external in stifling our doubts; for the review, apart from several excerpts which it offers, is largely a mere outline of the story. The method is contrary to Coleridge's, nor does the style betray any of his qualities.

The four reviews which we may now assign categorically to Coleridge are here for the first time identified as his. They are considerably earlier than any other of his recognized contributions in prose to periodical literature. They derive consequence from their collective concern with a species of literature then much in vogue. Also in two other respects a peculiar significance attaches to them.

(1) They confirm the impression that the romance of horror had an influence upon Coleridge's own work. His familiarity with Lewis's *Monk* and *Castle Spectre* has of course been known; and Mr. E. H. Coleridge once reminded me that the suggestion had been made that *Christabel* is indebted, both in imagery and in details of the plot, to *The Romance of the Forest* and *The Mysteries of Udolpho*.[1] The assurance we now have that Coleridge was widely acquainted with this type of fiction, and that he admired Mrs. Radcliffe above its other practitioners, makes the suggestion of his indebtedness more than credible. Personally I believe not only that his obligations may be traced in *Christabel* and *Osorio* ; but that *The Ancient Mariner*,

---

[1] See A. Brandl : *Samuel Taylor Coleridge and the English Romantic School* (1887), page 211 ff.; also E. H. Coleridge's edition of *Christabel* for the Royal Society of Literature (1907).

in its treatment of the supernatural, employs resources and avoids mistakes which its author had observed in the romances of horror.

(2) The reviews show further how much more quickly Coleridge developed as a critic than as a poet. The last three were written, it is true, not very much earlier than the greatest of his creative works; but we should also remember that they were written in advance even of *Osorio*, which certainly exhibits less fertility in its kind than they. If not equal to the best of his criticisms, they are at least recognizable as emanations of the same powerful and varied genius. They show the same ample, sometimes cumbersome, diction; the same felicity of phrase; here and there the same incisiveness that cuts in a dozen words to the very heart of the matter; here and there clear perceptions of ideas that were later to be expressed for all time; and almost the same breadth of outlook, the same depth of insight, the same powers of discrimination. Taken together, they constitute in themselves as illuminating a discussion of romantic *vs.* realistic fiction as we shall readily find. But the impression of the rapid maturity of Coleridge's critical faculties will be greatly strengthened if we consider the first of the reviews. Though of a piece with the others, it was published in August, 1794, and written we know not how much earlier than that date. Unquestionably it was composed several months before Coleridge's final separation from Cambridge. In other words a review which he would not have much altered or bettered even at the time of his criticism of Wordsworth belongs to his schoolboy days—to a period not only in advance of the sudden miraculous blossoming of his full poetical powers, but even in advance of his dreams of Pantisocracy and his verses " To a Young Ass."

Without further comment the criticisms may now be given precisely as they appeared in the *Critical Review.*

THE CRITICAL REVIEW, AUGUST, 1794, pp. 361–72

The Mysteries of Udolpho, a Romance ; interspersed with
some Pieces of Poetry. By Ann Radcliffe, Author of
the Romance of the Forest, &c. 4 *Vols.* Robinsons.
1794.

> 'Thine too these golden keys, immortal boy!
>   This can unlock the gates of joy,
>   Of horror, that and thrilling fears,
>   Or ope the sacred source of sympathetic tears.'

SUCH were the presents of the Muse to the infant
Shakespeare, and though perhaps to no other mortal
has she been so lavish of her gifts, the keys referring
to the third line Mrs. Radcliffe must be allowed to be
completely in possession of. This, all who have read
the Romance of the Forest will willingly bear witness
to. Nor does the present production require the name
of its author to ascertain that it comes from the same
hand. The same powers of description are displayed,
the same predilection is discovered for the wonderful
and the gloomy—the same mysterious terrors are
continually exciting in the mind the idea of a supernatural appearance, keeping us, as it were, upon the
very edge and confines of the world of spirits, and
yet are ingeniously explained by familiar causes;
curiosity is kept upon the stretch from page to page,
and from volume to volume, and the secret, which the
reader thinks himself every instant on the point of
penetrating, flies like a phantom before him, and
eludes his eagerness till the very last moment of pro-
tracted expectation. This art of escaping the guesses

of the reader has been improved and brought to perfection along with the reader's sagacity; just as the
various inventions of locks, bolts, and private drawers,
in order to secure, fasten, and hide, have always kept
pace with the ingenuity of the pickpocket and house-
breaker, whose profession is to unlock, unfasten, and
lay open what you have taken so much pains to conceal. In this contest of curiosity on one side, and
invention on the other, Mrs. Radcliffe has certainly
the advantage. She delights in concealing her plan
with the most artificial contrivance, and seems to
amuse herself with saying, at every turn and doubling
of the story, ' Now you think you have me, but I shall
take care to disappoint you.' This method is, however, liable to the following inconvenience, that in
the search of what is new, an author is apt to forget
what is natural; and, in rejecting the more obvious
conclusions, to take those which are less satisfactory.
The trite and the extravagant are the Scylla and
Charybdis of writers who deal in fiction. With
regard to the work before us, while we acknowledge
the extraordinary powers of Mrs. Radcliffe, some
readers will be inclined to doubt whether they have
been exerted in the present work with equal effect as
in the Romance of the Forest. Four volumes cannot
depend entirely on terrific incidents and intricacy of
story. They require character, unity of design, a
delineation of the scenes of real life, and the variety
of well supported contrast. The Mysteries of Udolpho
are indeed relieved by much elegant description and
picturesque scenery; but in the descriptions there is
too much of sameness: the pine and the larch tree
wave, and the full moon pours its lustre through
almost every chapter. Curiosity is raised oftener than
it is gratified; or rather, it is raised so high that no
adequate gratification can be given it; the interest is
completely dissolved when once the adventure is
finished, and the reader, when he is got to the end of

the work, looks about in vain for the spell which had
bound him so strongly to it.   There are other little
defects, which impartiality obliges us to notice.   The
manners do not sufficiently correspond with the aera
the author has chosen; which is the latter end of the
sixteenth century.   There is, perhaps, no direct
anachronism, but the style of accomplishments given
to the heroine, a country young lady, brought up on
the banks of the Garonne; the mention of botany;
of little circles of infidelity, &c. give so much the air
of modern manners, as is not counter-balanced by
Gothic arches and antique furniture.   It is possible
that the manners of different ages may not differ so
much as we are apt to imagine, and more than probable that we are generally wrong when we attempt to
delineate any but our own; but there is at least a
style of manners which our imagination has appro-
priated to each period, and which, like the costume of
theatrical dress, is not departed from without hurting
the feelings.—The character of Annette, a talkative
waiting-maid, is much worn, and that of the aunt,
madame Cheron, is too low and selfish to excite any
degree of interest, or justify the dangers her niece
exposes herself to for her sake.   We must likewise
observe, that the adventures do not sufficiently point
to one centre: we do not, however, attempt to analyse
the story; as it would have no other effect than destroying the pleasure of the reader, we shall content
ourselves with giving the following specimen of one
of those picturesque scenes of terror, which the author
knows so well to work up:

'During the remainder of the day, Emily's mind
was agitated with doubts and fears and contrary de-
terminations, on the subject of meeting this Barnardine
on the rampart, and submitting herself to his guidance,
she scarcely knew whither.   Pity for her aunt and
anxiety for herself alternately swayed her determination, and night came, before she had decided upon

her conduct. She heard the castle clock strike eleven
—twelve—and yet her mind wavered. The time,
however, was now come, when she could hesitate no
longer: and then the interest she felt for her aunt
overcame other considerations, and bidding Annette
follow her to the outer door of the vaulted gallery,
and there await her return, she descended from her
chamber. The castle was perfectly still, and the great
hall, where so lately she had witnessed a scene of
dreadful contention, now returned only the whispering
footsteps of the two solitary figures gliding fearfully
between the pillars, and gleamed only to the feeble
lamp they carried. Emily, deceived by the long
shadows of the pillars, and by the catching lights
between, often stopped, imagining she saw some person, moving in the distant obscurity of the perspective;
and, as she passed these pillars, she feared to turn her
eyes towards them, almost expecting to see a figure
start out from behind their broad shaft. She reached,
however, the vaulted gallery, without interruption,
but unclosed its outer door with a trembling hand,
and, charging Annette not to quit it, and to keep it a
little open, that she might be heard if she called, she
delivered to her the lamp, which she did not dare to
take herself because of the men on watch, and, alone,
stepped out upon the dark terrace. Every thing was
so still, that she feared lest her own light steps should
be heard by the distant sentinels, and she walked
cautiously towards the spot, where she had before met
Barnardine, listening for a sound, and looking onward
through the gloom in search of him. At length, she
was startled by a deep voice, that spoke near her, and
she paused, uncertain whether it was his, till it spoke
again, and she then recognized the hollow tones of
Barnardine, who had been punctual to the moment,
and was at the appointed place, resting on the rampart
wall. After chiding her for not coming sooner, and
saying, that he had been waiting nearly half an hour,

he desired Emily, who made no reply, to follow him
to the door through which he had entered the
terrace.

'While he unlocked it she looked back to that she
had left, and observing the rays of the lamp stream
through a small opening, was certain that Annette
was still there. But her remote situation could little
befriend Emily, after she had quitted the terrace; and,
when Barnardine unclosed the gate, the dismal aspect
of the passage beyond, shewn by a torch burning on
the pavement, made her shrink from following him
alone, and she refused to go, unless Annette might
accompany her. This, however, Barnardine absolutely refused to permit, mingling at the same time
with his refusal such artful circumstances to heighten
the pity and curiosity of Emily towards her aunt, that
she, at length, consented to follow him alone to the
portal.

'He then took up the torch, and led her along the
passage, at the extremity of which he unlocked
another door, whence they descended, a few steps,
into a chapel, which, as Barnardine held up the torch
to light her, Emily observed to be in ruins, and she
immediately recollected a former conversation of
Annette, concerning it, with very unpleasant emotions.
She looked fearfully on the almost roofless walls, green
with damps, and on the Gothic points of the windows,
where the ivy and the briony had long supplied the
place of glass, and ran mantling among the broken
capitals of some columns, that had once supported
the roof. Barnardine stumbled over the broken pavement, and his voice, as he uttered a sudden oath, was
returned in hollow echoes, that made it more terrific.
Emily's heart sunk: but she still followed him, and
he turned out of what had been the principle aisle of
the chapel. "Down these steps, lady," said Barnardine, as he descended a flight, which appeared to
lead into the vaults; but Emily paused on the top,

and demanded, in a tremulous tone, whither he was
conducting her.

" To the portal," said Barnardine.

" Cannot we go through the chapel to the portal ? "
said Emily.

" No, Signora; that leads to the inner court,
which I don't choose to unlock. This way, and we
shall reach the outer court presently."

Emily still hesitated; fearing not only to go on,
but, since she had gone thus far, to irritate Barnardine
by refusing to go further.

" Come, lady," said the man, who had nearly
reached the bottom of the flight, " make a little haste;
I cannot wait here all night."

" Whither do these steps lead ? " said Emily, yet
pausing.

" To the portal," repeated Barnardine, in an
angry tone, " I will wait no longer." As he said this,
he moved on with the light, and Emily, fearing to
provoke him by further delay, reluctantly followed.
From the steps, they proceeded through a passage
adjoining the vaults, the walls of which were dropping
with unwholesome dews, and the vapours, that crept
along the ground, made the torch burn so dimly, that
Emily expected every moment to see it extinguished,
and Barnardine could scarcely find his way. As they
advanced, these vapours thickened, and Barnardine
believing the torch was expiring, stopped for a moment
to trim it. As he then rested against a pair of iron
gates, that opened from the passage, Emily saw, by
uncertain flashes of light, the vaults beyond, and, near
her, heaps of earth, that seemed to surround an open
grave. Such an object, in such a scene, would, at any
time, have disturbed her; but now she was shocked
by an instantaneous presentiment, that this was the
grave of her unfortunate aunt, and that the treacherous
Barnardine was leading herself to destruction. The
obscure and terrible place, to which he had conducted

her, seemed to justify the thought; it was a place
suited for murder, a receptacle for the dead, where a
deed of horror might be committed, and no vestige
appear to proclaim it. Emily was so overwhelmed
with terror, that, for a moment, she was unable to
determine what conduct to pursue. She then considered, that it would be vain to attempt an escape
from Barnardine, by flight, since the length and the
intricacy of the way she had passed, would soon enable
him to overtake her, who was unacquainted with the
turnings, and whom feebleness would not enable her
to run long with swiftness. She feared equally to
irritate him by a disclosure of her suspicions, which a
refusal to accompany him further certainly would do;
and, since she was already as much in his power as
it was possible she could be, if she proceeded, she,
at length, determined to suppress, as far as she could,
the appearance of apprehension, and to follow silently
whither he designed to lead her. Pale with horror
and anxiety, she now waited till Barnardine had
trimmed the torch, and, as her sight glanced again
upon the grave, she could not forbear enquiring for
whom it was prepared. He took his eyes from the
torch, and fixed them upon her face without speaking.
She faintly repeated the question, but the man,
shaking the torch, passed on; and she followed,
trembling, to a second flight of steps; having ascended
which, a door delivered them into the first court of
the castle. As they crossed it, the light showed the
high black walls around them, fringed with long grass
and dank weeds, that found a scanty soil among the
mouldering stones; the heavy buttresses, with, here
and there, between them, a narrow grate, that admitted
a freer circulation of air to the court, the massy iron
gates that led to the castle, whose clustering turrets
appeared above, and, opposite, the huge towers and
arch of the portal itself. In this scene the large, un-
couth person of Barnardine, bearing the torch, formed

a characteristic figure. This Barnardine was wrapt in
a long dark cloak, which scarcely allowed the kind of
half-boots, or sandals, that were laced upon his legs,
to appear, and shewed only the point of a broad sword,
which he usually wore, slung in a belt across his
shoulders. On his head was a heavy flat velvet cap,
somewhat resembling a turban, in which was a short
feather; the visage beneath it shewed strong features,
and a countenance furrowed with the lines of cunning,
and darkened by habitual discontent.

'The view of the court, however, reanimated
Emily, who, as she crossed silently towards the
portal, began to hope, that her own fears, and not the
treachery of Barnardine, had deceived her. She looked
anxiously up at the first casement, that appeared above
the lofty arch of the portcullis; but it was dark, and
she enquired whether it belonged to the chamber,
where Madame Montoni was confined. Emily spoke
low, and Barnardine, perhaps, did not hear her question, for he returned no answer; and they, soon after,
entered the postern door of the gate-way, which
brought them to the foot of a narrow staircase, that
wound up one of the towers.

"Up this staircase the Signora lies," said Barnardine.

"Lies!" repeated Emily faintly, as she began to
ascend.

"She lies in the upper chamber," said Barnardine.

As they passed up, the wind, which poured through
the narrow cavities in the wall, made the torch flare,
and it threw a stronger gleam upon the grim and
sallow countenance of Barnardine, and discovered
more fully the desolation of the place—the rough
stone walls, the spiral stairs, black with age, and a
suit of ancient armour, with an iron visor, that hung
upon the walls, and appeared a trophy of some former
victory.

'Having reached a landing-place, "You may wait

here, lady," said he, applying a key to the door of a chamber, " while I go up, and tell the Signora you are coming."

" That ceremony is unnecessary," replied Emily, " my aunt will rejoice to see me."

"I am not so sure of that," said Barnardine, pointing to the room he had opened. " Come in here, lady, while I ſtep up."

' Emily, surprised and somewhat shocked, did not dare to oppose him further, but, as he was turning away with the torch, desired he would not leave her in darkness. He looked around, and, observing a tripod lamp, that stood on the ſtairs, lighted and gave it to Emily, who ſtepped forward into a large old chamber, and he closed the door. As she liſtened anxiously to his departing ſteps, she thought he descended, inſtead of ascended, the ſtairs; but the guſts of wind, that whiſtled round the portal, would not allow her to hear diſtinctly any other sound. Still, however, she liſtened, and, perceiving no ſtep in the room above, where he had affirmed Madame Montoni to be, her anxiety increased, though she considered that the thickness of the floor in this ſtrong building might prevent any sound reaching her from the upper chamber. The next moment, in a pause of the wind, she diſtinguished Barnardine's ſtep descending to the court, and then thought she heard his voice; but, the rising guſt again overcoming other sounds, Emily, to be certain on this point, moved softly to the door, which, on attempting to open it, she discovered was faſtened. All the horrid apprehensions, that had lately assailed her, returned at this inſtant with redoubled force, and no longer appeared like the exaggerations of a timid spirit, but seemed to have been sent to warn her of her fate. She now did not doubt, that Madame Montoni had been murdered, perhaps in this very chamber ; or that she herself was brought hither for the same purpose. The countenance, the manners, and the recollected words of Barnardine, when he had spoken of her aunt, confirmed her worst fears. For some moments, she was incapable of considering of any means, by which she might attempt an escape. Still she listened, but heard footsteps neither on the stairs nor in the room above; she thought, however, that she again distinguished Barnardine's voice below, and went to a grated window, that opened upon the court, to enquire further. Here, she plainly heard his hoarse accents, mingling with the blast, that swept by, but they were lost again so quickly, that their meaning could not be interpreted; and then the light of a torch, which seemed to issue from the portal below, flashed across the court, and the long shadow of a man, who was under the archway, appeared upon the pavement. Emily, from the hugeness of this sudden portrait, concluded it to be that of Barnardine; but other deep tones, which passed in the wind, soon convinced her he was not alone, and that his companion was not a person very liable to pity.

'When her spirits had overcome the first shock of her situation, she held up the lamp to examine if the chamber afforded a possibility of an escape. It was a spacious room, whose walls, wainscoted with rough oak, showed no casement but the grated one, which Emily had left, and no other door than that by which she had entered. The feeble rays of the lamp, however, did not allow her to see at once its full extent; she perceived no furniture, except, indeed, an iron chair, fastened in the centre of the chamber, immediately over which, depending on a chain from the ceiling, hung an iron ring. Having gazed upon these, for some time, with wonder and horror, she next observed iron bars below, made for the purpose of confining the feet, and on the arms of the chair were rings of the same metal. As she continued to survey them, she concluded that they were instruments of

N

torture, and it struck her, that some poor wretch had
once been fastened in this chair, and had there been
starved to death. She was chilled by the thought;
but, what was her agony when, in the next moment,
it occurred to her, that her aunt might have been one
of these victims, and that she herself might be the
next ! An acute pain seized her head, she was scarcely
able to hold the lamp, and, looking round for support,
she was seating herself, unconsciously, in the iron
chair itself; but suddenly perceiving where she was,
she started from it in horror, and sprung towards a
remote end of the room. Here again she looked round
for a seat to sustain her, and perceived only a dark
curtain, which, descending from the ceiling to the
floor, was drawn along the whole side of the chamber.
Ill as she was, the appearance of this curtain struck
her, and she paused to gaze upon it, in wonder and
apprehension.

' It seemed to conceal a recess of the chamber;
she wished, yet dreaded, to lift it, and to discover what
it veiled: twice she was withheld by a recollection of
the terrible spectacle her daring hand had formerly
unveiled in an apartment of the castle, till, suddenly
conjecturing that it concealed the body of her murdered aunt, she seized it, in a fit of desperation, and
drew it aside. Beyond, appeared a corpse, stretched
on a kind of low couch, which was crimsoned with
human blood, as was the floor beneath. The features,
deformed by death, were ghastly and horrible, and
more than one livid wound appeared in the face.
Emily, bending over the body, gazed, for a moment,
with an eager, frenzied eye; but, in the next, the lamp
dropped from her hand, and she fell senseless at the
foot of the couch.

' When her senses returned, she found herself
surrounded by men, among whom was Barnardine,
who was lifting her from the floor, and then bore her
along the chamber. She was sensible of what passed,

but the extreme languor of her spirits did not permit her to speak, or move, or even to feel any distinct fear. They carried her down the stair-case, by which she had ascended; when, having reached the arch-way, they stopped, and one of the men, taking the torch from Barnardine, opened a small door, that was cut in the great gate, and, as he stepped out upon the road, the light he bore shewed several men on horseback, in waiting. Whether it was the freshness of the air, that revived Emily, or that the objects she now saw roused the spirit of alarm, she suddenly spoke, and made an ineffectual effort to disengage herself from the grasp of the ruffians, who held her.

' Barnardine, meanwhile, called loudly for the torch, while distant voices answered, and several persons approached, and, in the same instant, a light flashed upon the court of the castle. Again he vociferated for the torch, and the men hurried Emily through the gate. At a short distance, under the shelter of the castle walls, she perceived the fellow, who had taken the light from the porter, holding it to a man, busily employed in altering the saddle of a horse, round which were several horsemen, looking on, whose harsh features received the full glare of the torch; while the broken ground beneath them, the opposite walls, with the tufted shrubs, that overhung their summits, and an embattled watch-tower above, were reddened with the gleam, which, fading gradually away, left the remoter ramparts and the woods below to the obscurity of night.

' " What do you waste time for, there ? " said Barnardine with an oath, as he approached the horsemen. " Dispatch—dispatch."

' " The saddle will be ready in a minute," replied the man who was buckling it, at whom Barnardine now swore again, for his negligence, and Emily, calling feebly for help, was hurried towards the horses, while the ruffians disputed on which to place her, the one

designed for her not being ready. At this moment a
cluster of lights issued from the great gates, and she
immediately heard the shrill voice of Annette above
those of several other persons, who advanced.   In
the same moment, she distinguished Montoni and
Cavigni, followed by a number of ruffian-faced fellows,
to whom she no longer looked with terror, but with
hope, for, at this instant, she did not tremble at the
thought of any dangers that might await her within
the castle, whence so lately and so anxiously she had
wished to escape.   Those, who threated her from
without, had engrossed all her apprehensions.

' A short contest ensued between the parties, in
which that of Montoni, however, were presently
victors, and the horsemen, perceiving that numbers
were against them, and being, perhaps, not very
warmly interested in the affair they had undertaken,
galloped off, while Barnardine had run far enough to
be lost in the darkness, and Emily was led back into
the castle.   As she re-passed the courts, the remembrance of what she had seen in the portal-chamber
came, with all its horror, to her mind; and when,
soon after, she heard the gate close, that shut her once
more within the castle walls, she shuddered for herself,
and, almost forgetting the danger she had escaped,
could scarcely think that any thing less precious than
liberty and peace was to be found beyond them.'

These volumes are interspersed with many pieces
of poetry, some beautiful, all pleasing, but rather
monotonous.   We cannot resist the temptation of
giving our readers the following charming one, more
especially as poetical beauties have not a fair chance
of being attended to, amidst the stronger interest
inspired by such a series of adventures.   The love of
poetry is a taste; curiosity is a kind of appetite, and
hurries headlong on, impatient for its complete
gratification :

'THE SEA-NYMPH.

' Down, down a thousand fathom deep,
Among the sounding seas I go;
Play round the foot of every steep
Whose cliffs above the ocean grow.

There, within their secret caves,
I hear the mighty rivers roar;
And guide their streams through Neptune's waves
To bless the green earth's inmost shore:

And bid the freshen'd waters glide,
For fern-crown'd nymphs of lake, or brook,
Through winding woods and pastures wide,
And many a wild, romantic nook.

For this the nymphs, at fall of eve,
Oft dance upon the flow'ry banks,
And sing my name, and garlands weave
To bear beneath the wave their thanks.

In coral bow'rs I love to lie,
And hear the surges roll above,
And through the waters view on high
The proud ships sail, and gay clouds move.

And oft at midnight's stillest hour,
When summer seas the vessel lave,
I love to prove my charmful pow'r
While floating on the moon-light wave.

And when deep sleep the crew has bound,
And the sad lover musing leans
O'er the ship's side, I breathe around
Such strains as speak no mortal means!

O'er the dim waves his searching eye
Sees but the vessel's lengthen'd shade;
Above—the moon and azure sky;
Entranc'd he hears, and half afraid!

Sometimes, a single note I swell,
That, softly sweet, at distance dies;
Then wake the magic of my shell,
And choral voices round me rise!

The trembling youth, charm'd by my strain,
Calls up the crew, who, silent, bend
O'er the high deck, but list in vain;
My song is hush'd, my wonders end![1]

Within the mountain's woody bay,
Where the tall bark at anchor rides,
At twilight hour, with tritons gay,
I dance upon the lapsing tides:

And with my sister-nymphs I sport,
Till the broad sun looks o'er the floods;[2]
Then, swift we seek our crystal court,
Deep in the wave, 'mid Neptune's woods.

---

[1] I cannot help believing that these stanzas contributed something to the exquisite passage in Part V of *The Ancient Mariner* :

" Slowly the sounds came back again,
Now mixed, now one by one.

" Sometimes a-dropping from the sky
I heard the sky-lark sing;
Sometimes all little birds that are,
How they seemed to fill the sea and air
With their sweet jargoning !

" And now 'twas like all instruments,
Now like a lonely flute;
And now it is an angel's song,
That makes the heavens be mute.

" It ceased; yet still the sails made on
A pleasant noise till noon,
A noise like of a hidden brook
In the leafy month of June,
That to the sleeping woods all night
Singeth a quiet tune."

[2] Coleridge also refers (*The Ancient Mariner*, Part III) to the magnified appearance of the sun when it is near the watery horizon :

" Almost upon the western wave
Rested the broad bright sun."

In cool arcades and glassy halls,
We pass the sultry hours of noon,
Beyond wherever sun-beam falls,
Weaving sea-flowers in gay festoon.

The while we chant our ditties sweet
To some soft shell that warbles near;
Join'd by the murmuring current, fleet,
That glide along our halls so clear.

There, the pale pearl and sapphire blue,
And ruby red, and em'rald green,
Dart from the domes a changing hue,
And sparry columns deck the scene.

When the dark storm scowls o'er the deep,
And long, long peals of thunder sound,
On some high cliff my watch I keep
O'er all the restless seas around:

Till on the ridgy wave afar
Comes the lone vessel, labouring slow,
Spreading the white foam in the air,
With sail and top-mast bending low.

Then, plunge I mid the ocean's roar,
My way by quiv'ring lightnings shewn,
To guide the bark to peaceful shore,[1]
And hush the sailor's fearful groan.

And if too late I reach its side
To save it from the 'whelming surge,
I call my dolphins o'er the tide,
To bear the crew where isles emerge.

Their mournful spirits soon I cheer,
While round the desert coast I go,
With warbled songs they faintly hear,
Oft as the stormy gust sinks low.

[1] In *The Ancient Mariner* the ship is propelled by a spirit that
slides through the water:
  " Under the keel nine fathom deep."

My music leads to lofty groves,
That wild upon the sea-bank wave;
Where sweet fruits bloom, and fresh spring roves,
And closing boughs the tempeſt brave.

Then, from the air spirits obey
My potent voice they love so well,
And, on the clouds, paint visions gay,
While ſtrains more sweet at diſtance swell.

And thus the lonely hours I cheat,
Soothing the ship-wreck'd sailor's heart,
Till from the waves the ſtorms retreat,
And o'er the eaſt the day-beams dart.

Neptune for this oft binds me faſt
To rocks below, with choral chain,
Till all the tempeſt's over-paſt,
And drowning seamen cry in vain.

Whoe'er ye are that love my lay,
Come, when red sun-set tints the wave,
To the ſtill sands, where fairies play;
There, in cool seas, I love to lave.'

If, in consequence of the criticisms impartiality
has obliged us to make upon this novel, the author
should feel disposed to ask us, Who will write a better?
we boldly answer her, *Yourself ;* when no longer disposed to sacrifice excellence to quantity, and lengthen
out a ſtory for the sake of filling an additional volume.

III

THE CRITICAL REVIEW, JUNE, 1798, pp. 166–9

*The Italian, or the Confessional of the Black Penitents.
A Romance. By Ann Radcliffe, Author of the
Mysteries of Udolpho, &c. 3 Vols.* Cadell *and*
Davies. 1797.

IT was not difficult to foresee that the *modern romance*,
even supported by the skill of the most ingenious of
its votaries, would soon experience the fate of every
attempt to please by what is unnatural, and by a
departure from that observance of real life, which
has placed the works of Fielding, Smollett, and some
other writers, among the permanent sources of amusement. It might for a time afford an acceptable
variety to persons whose reading is confined to works
of fiction, and who would, perhaps, be glad to exchange dullness for extravagance; but it was probable
that, as its constitution (if we may so speak) was
maintained only by the passion of terror, and that
excited by trick, and as it was not conversant in
incidents and characters of a natural complexion, it
would degenerate into repetition, and would disappoint curiosity. So many cries ' that the wolf is
coming,' must at last lose their effect. In reviewing
the Mysteries of Udolpho, we hazarded an opinion,
that, if a better production could appear, it must come
only from the pen of Mrs. Radcliffe; but we were
not totally blind to the difficulties which even she
would have to encounter, in order to keep up the
interest she had created in that work, and in the
Romance of the Forest; and the present publication
confirms our suspicions. The Mysteries of Udolpho

fell short of the Romance of the Forest, by the tedious
protraction of events, and by a redundancy of description : the Italian falls short of the Mysteries of
Udolpho, by reminding us of the same characters and
the same scenes; and, although the descriptive part
is less prolix, the author has had recourse to it in
various instances, in which it has no natural connexion
with the story.   There are, however, some scenes that
powerfully seize the imagination, and interest the
passions.   Among these we prefer the interview
between the marchesa and Schedoni in the church,
and the discovery made by Schedoni that Ellena was
his daughter.   On the latter subject, we will gratify
our readers with an extract.   Schedoni approached
Ellena with an intention of murdering her; but,
' as often as he prepared to plunge the poignard in
her bosom, a shuddering horror restrained him.
Astonished at his own feelings, and indignant at what
he termed a dastardly weakness, he found it necessary
to argue with himself, and his rapid thoughts said,
" Do I not feel the necessity of this act !   Does not
what is dearer to me than existence—does not my
consequence depend on the execution of it ?   Is she
not also beloved by the young Vivaldi ?—have I
already forgotten the church of the Spirito Santo ? "
This consideration re-animated him; vengeance nerved
his arm, and drawing aside the lawn from her bosom,
he once more raised it to strike; when, after gazing
for an instant, some new cause of horror seemed to
seize all his frame, and he stood for some moments
aghast and motionless like a statue.   His respiration
was short and laborious, chilly drops stood on his
forehead, and all his faculties of mind seemed sus-
pended.   When he recovered, he stooped to examine
again the miniature, which had occasioned this revolu-
tion, and which had lain concealed beneath the lawn
that he withdrew.   The terrible certainty was almost
confirmed, and forgetting, in his impatience to know

the truth, the imprudence of suddenly discovering himself to Ellena at this hour of the night, and with a dagger at his feet, he called loudly "Awake! awake! Say, what is your name? Speak! speak quickly!"

‘ Ellena, aroused by a man's voice, started from her mattress, when, perceiving Schedoni, and, by the pale glare of the lamp, his haggard countenance, she shrieked, and sunk back on the pillow. She had not fainted; and believing that he came to murder her, she now exerted herself to plead for mercy. The energy of her feelings enabled her to rise and throw herself at his feet, "Be merciful, O father! be merciful!" said she, in a trembling voice.

"Father!" interrupted Schedoni, with earnestness; and then, seeming to restrain himself, he added, with unaffected surprise, "Why are you thus terrified?" for he had lost, in new interests and emotions, all consciousness of evil intention, and of the singularity of his situation. "What do you fear?" he repeated.

"Have pity, holy father!" exclaimed Ellena in agony.

"Why do you not say whose portrait that is?" demanded he, forgetting that he had not asked the question before.

"Whose portrait?" repeated the confessor in a loud voice.

"Whose portrait!" said Ellena, with extreme surprise.

"Ay, how came you by it? Be quick——whose resemblance is it?"

"Why should you wish to know?" said Ellena.

"Answer my question," repeated Schedoni, with increasing sternness.

"I cannot part with it, holy father," replied Ellena, pressing it to her bosom, "you do not wish me to part with it!"

"Is it impossible to make you answer my question?" said he, in extreme perturbation, and turning away from her, "has fear utterly confounded you!" Then, again stepping towards her, and seizing her wrist, he repeated the demand in a tone of desperation.

"Alas! he is dead! or I should not now want a protector," replied Ellena, shrinking from his grasp, and weeping.

"You trifle," said Schedoni, with a terrible look, "I once more demand an answer—whose picture?"

'Ellena lifted it, gazed upon it for a moment, and then pressing it to her lips said, "This was my father."

"Your father!" he repeated in an inward voice, "your father!" and shuddering, turned away.

'Ellena looked at him with surprise. "I never knew a father's care," she said, "nor till lately did I perceive the want of it.—But now."—

"His name?" interrupted the confessor.

"But now," continued Ellena—"if you are not as a father to me—to whom can I look for protection?"

"His name?" repeated Schedoni, with sterner emphasis.

"It is sacred," replied Ellena, "for he was unfortunate!"

"His name?" demanded the confessor, furiously.

"I have promised to conceal it, father."

"On your life, I charge you to tell it; remember, on your life!"

'Ellena trembled, was silent, and with supplicating looks implored him to desist from enquiry, but he urged the question more irresistibly. "His name then," said she, "was Marinella."

'Schedoni groaned and turned away; but in a few seconds, struggling to command the agitation that shattered his whole frame, he returned to Ellena, and raised her from her knees, on which she had thrown herself to implore mercy.

"The place of his residence?" said the monk.

" It was far from hence," she replied; but he demanded an unequivocal answer, and she reluctantly gave one.

' Schedoni turned away as before, groaned heavily, and paced the chamber without speaking; while Ellena, in her turn, enquired the motive of his questions, and the occasion of his agitation. But he seemed not to notice any thing she said, and, wholly given up to his feelings, was inflexibly silent, while he stalked, with measured steps, along the room, and his face, half hid by his cowl, was bent towards the ground.

' Ellena's terror began to yield to astonishment, and this emotion increased, when, Schedoni approaching her, she perceived tears swell in his eyes, which were fixt on her's, and his countenance soften from the wild disorder that had marked it. Still he could not speak. At length he yielded to the fulness of his heart, and Schedoni, the stern Schedoni, wept and sighed ! He seated himself on the mattress beside Ellena, took her hand, which she affrighted attempted to withdraw, and when he could command his voice, said, " Unhappy child !—behold your more unhappy father ! " As he concluded, his voice was overcome by groans, and he drew the cowl entirely over his face.' Vol. II, p. 294.

Among those parts of the romance which we disapprove, we may reckon the examination before the court of inquisition: it is so improbable, that we should rather have attributed it to one of Mrs. Radcliffe's numerous imitators.

But, notwithstanding occasional objections, the Italian may justly be considered as an ingenious performance; and many persons will read it with great pleasure and satisfaction.

IV

THE CRITICAL REVIEW, AUGUST, 1798, p. 472

Hubert de Sevrac. A Romance, of the 18th Century. By Mary Robinson, Author of Poems, Angelina, &c. 3 Vols. Hookham. 1796.

THE character of Mrs. Robinson's novels being generally known, it is perhaps sufficient to say, that Hubert de Sevrac is inferior to her former productions. It is an imitation of Mrs. Radcliffe's romances, but without any resemblance that may not be attained by a common pen. There are detached parts, however, of which we may speak with approbation; and, during the prevalence of the present taste for romances, the whole may afford amusement to the supporters of circulating libraries. But it may be necessary to apprise novel-writers, in general, that this taste is declining, and that real life and manners will soon assert their claims.

V

THE CRITICAL REVIEW, FEBRUARY, 1797, pp. 194–200

The Monk. A Romance. By M. G. Lewis, Esq. M.P.
    3 *Vols.* Bell. 1796.

THE horrible and the preternatural have usually seized
on the popular taste, at the rise and decline of literature. Most powerful stimulants, they can never be
required except by the torpor of an unawakened, or
the languor of an exhausted, appetite. The same
phaenomenon, therefore, which we hail as a favourable omen in the belles lettres of Germany, impresses
a degree of gloom in the compositions of our country-
men. We trust, however, that satiety will banish
what good sense should have prevented; and that,
wearied with fiends, incomprehensible characters,
with shrieks, murders, and subterraneous dungeons,
the public will learn, by the multitude of the manu-
facturers, with how little expense of thought or
imagination this species of composition is manufac-
tured. But, cheaply as we estimate romances in
general, we acknowledge, in the work before us, the
offspring of no common genius. The tale is similar
to that of Santon Barsista in the Guardian. Ambrosio,
a monk, surnamed the Man of Holiness, proud of
his own undeviating rectitude, and severe to the faults
of others, is successfully assailed by the tempter of
mankind, and seduced to the perpetration of rape and
murder, and finally precipitated into a contract in
which he consigns his soul to everlasting perdition.
    The larger part of the three volumes is occupied
by the underplot, which, however, is skilfully and

closely conne&ed with the main &ory, and is sub-
servient to its development.   The tale of the bleeding
nun is truly terrific; and we could not easily recolle&
a bolder or more happy conception than that of the
burning cross on the forehead of the wandering Jew
(a my&erious chara&er, which, though copied as to
its more prominent features from Schiller's incomprehensible Armenian, does, nevertheless, display
great vigour of fancy).   But the chara&er of Matilda,
the chief agent in the sedu&ion of Antonio,[1] appears
to us to be the author's ma&er-piece.   It is, indeed,
exquisitely imagined, and as exquisitely supported.
The whole work is di&inguished by the variety and
impressiveness of its incidents; and the author every-
where discovers an imagination rich, powerful, and
fervid.   Such are the excellencies;—the errors and
defe&s are more numerous, and (we are sorry to add)
of greater importance.

All events are levelled into one common mass, and
become almo& equally probable, where the order of
nature may be changed wherever the author's purposes demand it.   No address is requisite to the accom-
plishment of any design; and no pleasure therefore
can be received from the perception of *difficulty sur-
mounted.*   The writer may make us wonder, but he
cannot surprise us.   For the same reasons a romance
is incapable of exemplifying a moral truth.   No proud
man, for in&ance, will be made less proud by being
told that Lucifer once seduced a presumptuous monk.
Incredulus odit.   Or even if, believing the &ory, he
should deem his virtue less secure, he would yet acquire
no lessons of prudence, no feelings of humility.
Human prudence can oppose no sufficient shield to
the power and cunning of supernatural beings; and
the privilege of being proud might be fairly conceded
to him who could rise superior to all earthly temptations, and whom the strength of the spiritual world

[1] A misprint for Ambrosio.

alone would be adequate to overwhelm. So falling, he would fall with glory, and might reasonably welcome his defeat with the haughty emotions of a conqueror. As far, therefore, as the story is concerned, the praise which a romance can claim, is simply that of having given pleasure during its perusal; and so many are the calamities of life, that he who has done this, has not written uselessly. The children of sickness and of solitude shall thank him.—To this praise, however, our author has not entitled himself. The sufferings which he describes are so frightful and intolerable, that we break with abruptness from the delusion, and indignantly suspect the man of a species of brutality, who could find a pleasure in wantonly imagining them; and the abominations which he pourtrays with no hurrying pencil, are such as the observation of character by no means demanded, such as ' no observation of character can justify, because no good man would willingly suffer them to pass, however transiently, through his own mind.' The merit of a novelist is in proportion (not simply to the effect, but) to the *pleasurable* effect which he produces. Situations of torment, and images of naked horror, are easily conceived; and a writer in whose works they abound, deserves our gratitude almost equally with him who should drag us by way of sport through a military hospital, or force us to sit at the dissecting-table of a natural philosopher. To trace the nice boundaries, beyond which terror and sympathy are deserted by the pleasurable emotions,—to reach those limits, yet never to pass them,—*hic labor, hic opus est.* Figures that shock the imagination, and narratives that mangle the feelings, rarely discover *genius,* and always betray a low and vulgar *taste.* Nor has our author indicated less ignorance of the human heart in the management of the principal character. The wisdom and goodness of providence have ordered that the tendency of vicious actions to deprave the heart

o

of the perpetrator, should diminish in proportion to the greatness of his temptations. Now, in addition to constitutional warmth and irresistible opportunity, the monk is impelled to incontinence by friendship, by compassion, by gratitude, by all that is amiable, and all that is estimable; yet in a few weeks after his first frailty, the man who had been described as possessing much general humanity, a keen and vigorous understanding, with habits of the most exalted piety, degenerates into an uglier fiend than the gloomy imagination of Dante would have ventured to picture. Again, the monk is described as feeling and acting under the influence of an appetite which could not co-exist with his other emotions. The romance-writer possesses an unlimited power over situations; but he must scrupulously make his characters act in congruity with them. Let him work *physical* wonders only, and we will be content to *dream* with him for a while; but the first *moral* miracle which he attempts, he disgusts and awakens us. Thus our judgment remains unoffended, when, announced by thunders and earthquakes, the spirit appears to Ambrosio involved in blue fires that increase the cold of the cavern; and we acquiesce in the power of the silver myrtle which made gates and doors fly open at its touch, and charmed every eye into sleep. But when a mortal, fresh from the impression of that terrible appearance, and in the act of evincing for the first time the witching force of this myrtle, is represented as being at the same moment agitated by so fleeting an appetite as that of lust, our own feelings convince us that this is not improbable, but impossible; not preternatural, but contrary to nature. The extent of the powers that may exist, we can never ascertain; and therefore we feel no great difficulty in yielding a temporary belief to any, the strangest, situation of *things*. But that situation once conceived, how beings like ourselves would feel and act in it, our own feelings sufficiently

instruct us; and we instantly reject the clumsy fiction
that does not harmonise with them. These are the
two *principal* mistakes in *judgment*, which the author
has fallen into; but we cannot wholly pass over the
frequent incongruity of his style with his subjects. It
is gaudy where it should have been severely simple;
and too often the mind is offended by phrases the
most trite and colloquial, where it demands and had
expected a sternness and solemnity of diction.

A more grievous fault remains,—a fault for which
no literary excellence can atone,—a fault which all
other excellence does but aggravate, as adding
subtlety to a poison by the elegance of its prepara-
tion. Mildness of censure would here be criminally
misplaced, and silence would make us accomplices.
Not without reluctance then, but in full conviction
that we are performing a duty, we declare it to be
our opinion, that the Monk is a romance, which if a
parent saw in the hands of a son or daughter, he
might reasonably turn pale. The temptations of
Ambrosio are described with a libidinous minuteness,
which, we sincerely hope, will receive its best and
only adequate censure from the offended conscience
of the author himself. The shameless harlotry of
Matilda, and the trembling innocence of Antonia,
are seized with equal avidity, as vehicles of the most
voluptuous images; and though the tale is indeed a
tale of horror, yet the most painful impression which
the work left on our minds was that of great acquirements and splendid genius employed to furnish a
mormo for children, a poison for youth, and a provo-
cative for the debauchee. Tales of enchantments and
witchcraft can never be *useful*: our author has con-
trived to make them *pernicious*, by blending, with an
irreverent negligence, all that is most awfully true in
religion with all that is most ridiculously absurd in
superstition. He takes frequent occasion, indeed, to
manifest his sovereign contempt for the latter, both

in his own person, and (most incongruously) in that
of his principal characters; and that his respect for
the *former* is not excessive, we are forced to conclude
from the treatment which its inspired writings receive
from him.   Ambrosio discovers Antonia reading—

> 'He examined the book which she had been
> reading, and had now placed upon the table.   It
> was the Bible.
> "How!" said the friar to himself, "Antonia
> reads the Bible, and is still so ignorant?"
> 'But, upon a further inspection, he found that
> Elvira had made exactly the same remark.   That
> prudent mother, while she admired the beauties of
> the sacred writings, was convinced that, unre-
> stricted, no reading more improper could be per-
> mitted a young woman.   Many of the narratives
> can only tend to excite ideas the worst calculated
> for a female breast: every thing is called plainly
> and roundly by its name; and the *annals of a brothel*
> *would scarcely furnish a greater choice of indecent*
> *expressions*.   Yet this is the book which young
> women are recommended to study, which is put
> into the hands of children, able to comprehend
> little more than those passages of which they had
> better remain ignorant, and which but too *fre-*
> *quently inculcates the first rudiments of vice*, and gives
> the first alarm to the still sleeping passions.   Of
> this was Elvira so fully convinced, that she would
> have preferred putting into her daughter's hands
> "Amadis de Gaul," or "The Valiant Champion,
> Tirante the White"; and *would sooner have*
> *authorised her studying the lewd exploits of Don Galaor,*
> *or the lascivious jokes of the Damsel Plazer di mi vida.*'
> Vol. II, p. 247.

The impiety of this falsehood can be equalled only
by its impudence.   This is indeed as if a Corinthian
harlot, clad from head to foot in the transparent thinness

of the Cöan veſt, should affeſt to view with prudish horror the naked knee of a Spartan matron ! If it be possible that the author of these blasphemies is a Chriſtian, should he not have refleſted that the only passage in the scriptures,[1] which could give a *shadow* of plausibility to the *weakeſt* of these expressions, is represented as being spoken by the Almighty himself ? But if he be an infidel, he has aſted consiſtently enough with that charaſter, in his endeavours firſt to influence the fleshly appetites, and then to pour contempt on the only book which would be adequate to the task of recalming them.   We believe it not absolutely impossible that a mind may be so deeply depraved by the habit of reading lewd and voluptuous tales, as to use even the Bible in conjuring up the spirit of uncleanness.   The most innocent expressions might become the firſt link in the chain of association, when a man's soul had been so poisoned ; and we believe it not absolutely impossible that he might extraſt pollution from the word of purity, and, in a literal sense, *turn the grace of God into wantonness.*

We have been induced to pay particular attention to this work, from the unusual success which it has experienced.   It certainly possesses much real merit, in addition to its meretricious attraſtions.   Nor muſt it be forgotten that the author is a man of rank and fortune.—Yes ! the author of the Monk signs himself a LEGISLATOR !—We ſtare and tremble.

The poetry interspersed through the volumes is, in general, far above mediocrity.   We shall present our readers with the following exquisitely tender elegy, which, we may venture to prophesy, will melt and delight the heart, when ghoſts and hobgoblins shall be found only in the lumber-garret of a circulating library.

[1] Ezekiel, chap. XXIII.   [Coleridge's note.]

"THE EXILE

' Farewell, oh native Spain! farewell for ever!
These banished eyes shall view thy coasts no more:
A mournful presage tells my heart, that never
Gonzalvo's steps again shall press thy shore.

' Hushed are the winds; while soft the vessel sailing
With gentle motion plows the unruffled main,
I feel my bosom's boasted courage failing,
And curse the waves which bear me far from Spain.

' I see it yet!   Beneath yon blue clear heaven
Still do the spires, so well-beloved, appear.
From yonder craggy point the gale of even
Still wafts my native accents to mine ear.

' Propped on some moss-crowned rock, and gaily singing,
There in the sun his nets the fisher dries;
Oft have I heard the plaintive ballad, bringing
Scenes of past joys before my sorrowing eyes.

' Ah! happy swain! he waits the accustomed hour,
When twilight-gloom obscures the closing sky;
Then gladly seeks his loved paternal bower,
And shares the feast his native fields supply.

' Friendship and Love, his cottage guests, receive him
With honest welcome and with smile sincere:
No threatening woes of present joys bereave him;
No sigh his bosom owns, his cheek no tear.

' Ah! happy swain! such bliss to me denying,
Fortune thy lot with envy bids me view;
Me, who, from home and Spain an exile flying,
Bid all I value, all I love, adieu.

' No more mine ear shall list the well-known ditty
Sung by some mountain-girl, who tends her goats,
Some village-swain imploring amorous pity,
Or shepherd chanting wild his rustic notes.

'No more my arms a parent's fond embraces,
No more my heart domestic calm must know;
Far from these joys, with sighs which memory traces,
To sultry skies and distant climes I go.

'Where Indian suns engender new diseases,
Where snakes and tigers breed, I bend my way,
To brave the feverish thirst no art appeases,
The yellow plague, and madding blaze of day.

'But not to feel slow pangs consume my liver,
To die by piece-meal in the bloom of age,
My boiling blood drank by insatiate fever,
And brain delirious with the day-star's rage,

'Can make me know such grief, as thus to sever,
With many a bitter sigh, dear land! from thee;
To feel this heart must dote on thee for ever,
And feel that all thy joys are torn from me!

'Ah me! how oft will fancy's spells, in slumber,
Recall my native country to my mind!
How oft regret will bid me sadly number
Each lost delight, and dear friend left behind!

'Wild Murcia's vales and loved romantic bowers,
The river on whose banks a child I played,
My castle's antient halls, its frowning towers,
Each much-regretted wood, and well-known glade;

'Dreams of the land where all my wishes centre,
Thy scenes, which I am doomed no more to know,
Full oft shall memory trace, my soul's tormentor,
And turn each pleasure past to present woe.

'But, lo! the sun beneath the waves retires;
Night speeds apace her empire to restore!
Clouds from my sight obscure the village-spires,
Now seen but faintly, and now seen no more.

'Oh, breathe not, winds! Still be the water's motion!
Sleep, sleep, my bark, in silence on the main!
So, when to-morrow's light shall gild the ocean,
Once more mine eyes shall see the coast of Spain.

'Vain is the wish! My last petition scorning,
Fresh blows the gale, and high the billows swell:
Far shall we be before the break of morning:
Oh! then, for ever, native Spain, farewell!'

Vol. II, p. 165.

INDEX